Collins

Incredible Earth 2

Meenakshi Atal
Debahuti Das

Components of DigiSuite

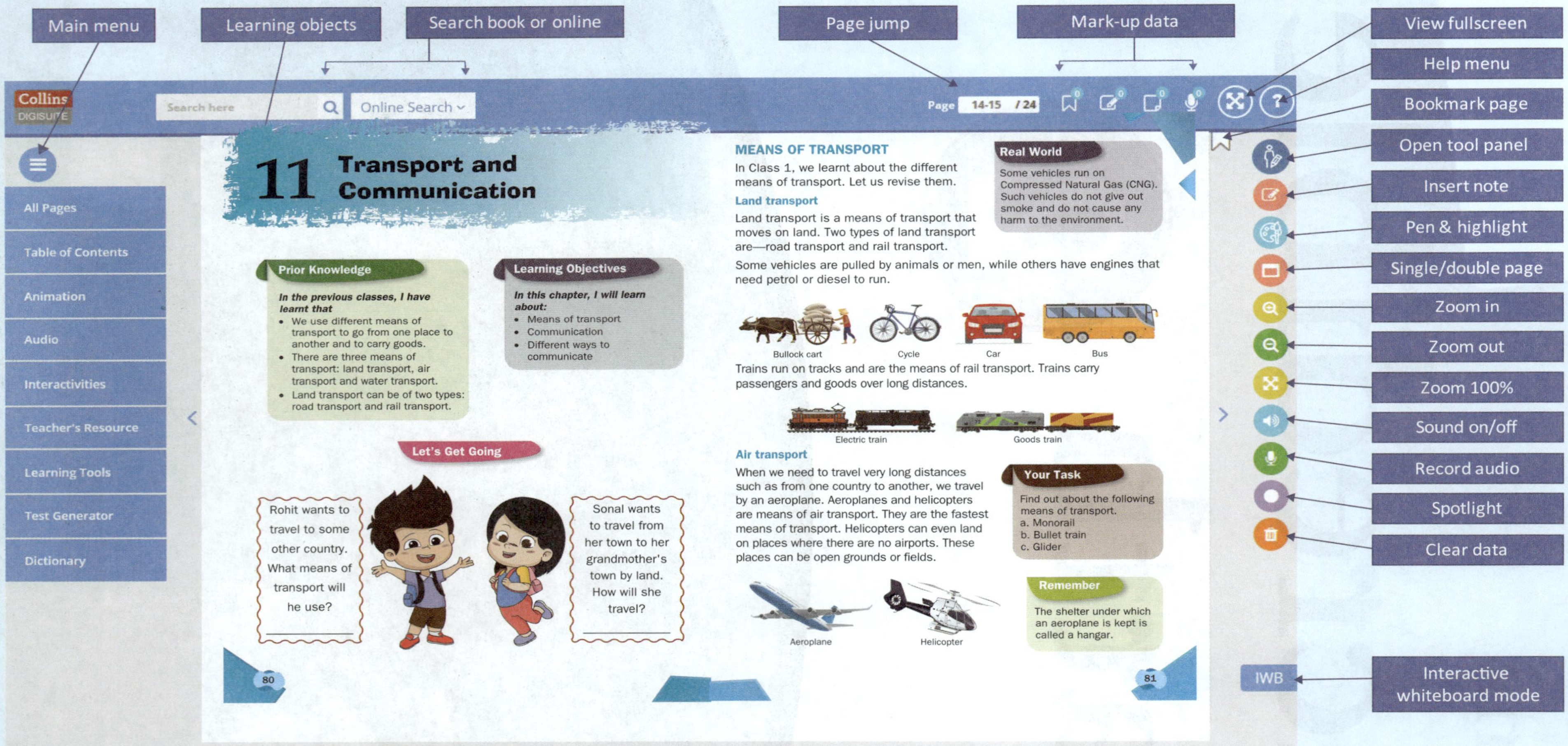

Student + Teacher			Teacher-only	
animations	ia activities	g games	lp lesson plans	tn teacher's notes
ilt instructor-led tutorials	w worksheets	v videos	w worksheets	ak answer keys
	audio			

Preface

Collins *Incredible* is a series of eight books for Classes 1 to 8. **Collins *Incredible Earth 1 and 2*** have been designed considering the multidisciplinary nature of Environmental Studies. **Collins *Incredible Science 3 to 8*** are focused on developing scientific skills and their application in real life.

This series adheres to the guidelines of the *National Education Policy (NEP) 2020* and aligns with the vision of the *National Initiative for Proficiency in Reading with Understanding and Numeracy* (NIPUN Bharat). It adopts the *5E Learning Model* and follows a thematic, coherent and structured approach, effectively integrating subject knowledge, NEP elements such as Experiential Learning, Art Integration, Cross-Curricular and India Focus and *21st Century Skills* for the overall development of the students. The series also aims to make the students aware of the *Sustainable Development Goals* (SDGs) of the United Nations so that they can become SDG Pioneers, Champions or Ambassadors.

SAFAL in **Collins *Incredible Series*:** This series also strives to make a shift from rote-learning to competency-based learning, in accordance with Structured Assessment For Analyzing Learning (SAFAL). The components of SAFAL—critical thinking, inquiry-based learning and analysis-based learning—are woven into the features such as Skills Enrichment Zone, Worksheets, the latest National Science Olympiad Paper, SEE Learning, Earth/Science Fair and Khagol Talim (Astronomy Education) Worksheets.

We would like to take this opportunity to thank all the teachers who reviewed the books and provided their invaluable feedback.

Any suggestions or constructive criticism from the users are welcome. We shall try to incorporate those in future editions.

Authors

About the Authors

Meenakshi Atal, former Vice Principal of The Heritage School, Kolkata, is an eminent educationist and teacher trainer with over four decades of experience.

Debahuti Das of The Heritage School, Kolkata, has a teaching career extending over two decades and has been a pioneer in evolving innovative methods of teaching.

Key Features

The key features of **Collins Incredible Series** are completely aligned with the *National Education Policy (NEP) 2020* and the vision of the *National Initiative for Proficiency in Reading with Understanding and Numeracy* (NIPUN Bharat). These meticulously designed features, based on the *5E Learning Model*, can be used as learning strategies to help in the overall development of scientific and *21st Century Skills* in students. These key features also aim to help the learners shift from rote-learning to competency-based learning, in accordance with *Structured Assessment For Analyzing Learning* (SAFAL).

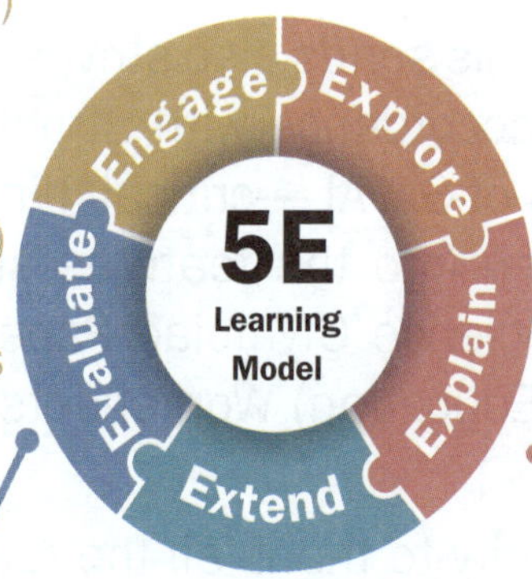

Engage — To capture the attention of students, get them mentally engaged and make connections between past and present

- I Am a Scientist! (Classes 3 to 8)
- Prior knowledge
- Let's Get Going
- Real World
- Science in Action (Classes 3 to 8)
- Concept Map
- Eminent Personalities/Scientists
- Picture Story

Explore — To enable the students to explore the concepts through hands-on activities, investigations, etc.

- Nature Trail/Science Around Us
- Let's Investigate (Classes 6 to 8)
- Tech Updates (Classes 3 to 8)
- Talk About (Classes 1 to 5)
- Your Task
- Let's Try
- SEE Learning
- Earth/Science Fair

Explain — To enable the students to understand the main ideas of the topics

- Learning Objectives
- Remember
- My Dictionary
- Summary
- Keywords (Classes 3 to 8)

Extend — To enable the students to stimulate thinking and apply prior and current knowledge to real-life situations

- Skills Enrichment Zone
- Worksheets

Evaluate — To review, assess and evaluate what students have learned

- Knowledge Check
- Practice Zone
- Review Corner

Adherence to National Education Policy

21st Century Skills (21 CS)

Learning Skills
- Critical Thinking
- Creativity and Innovation
- Collaboration
- Communication

Life Skills
- Flexibility and Adaptability
- Leadership and Responsibility
- Initiative and Self-Direction
- Productivity and Accountability
- Social and Cross-Cultural Interaction

Literacy Skills
- Information Literacy
- Media Literacy
- Technology Literacy

Art Integration (AI)

Cross Curricular (CC)

India Focus (IF)

Happiness Quotient (HQ)

Experiential Learning (EL)

SUSTAINABLE DEVELOPMENT GOALS

Each feature has been tagged with colour-coded icons to easily identify the type of skills and learning being addressed!

About the Features

To connect environmental studies/science with Indian history, art, culture and real-life situations

Selective topics that would serve as the basics to becoming a scientist

Interesting project ideas and thought-provoking questions to address the main elements of NEP 2020

Interesting project ideas integrating Science, Technology, Engineering, Arts and Mathematics to solve real-world problems

Sample test papers for review and assessment (Classes 6 to 8 Assessment Corner based on the **New Assessment format)**

Colourful cartoon spreads based on environmental awareness

Special stories to promote social, emotional and ethical learning

Innovative projects and model-making ideas that can be displayed in various school events

Brief write-up on the contributions of a few eminent personalities/ scientists

Informative and interactive colourful posters to focus on some important concepts or facts

Contents

Nature Trail
Waste Art in India

The waste generated by us daily is a great threat to us and our nature. With the increase in population, the amount of waste generated is also increasing in India. There are many artists who recycle it to form eye-catching works of art.

Rock garden in Chandigarh, India made by Nek Chand out of industrial and home waste and thrown-away items

The Mad Crab of Kochi, an art with Waste Plastics

Various waste items can be recycled to form different art forms.

Hanging flower pot made of plastic bottle

Toy car made of paper carton

Find out about the lion art of 'MAKE IN INDIA' logo. Who created it and how? With the help of an elder, collect some pictures of this art form and paste them in the space provided below.

Find out about some DIY crafts that can be created using various waste items. Try them out and paste their pictures in the space provided below.

I Am Special!

DO YOU WANT TO KNOW ME?

My name is ____________________.

I am a __________ (boy/girl).

My birthday is on ____________________.

I am __________ years old.

I live with my ____________________

My school ____________________

The city I live in ____________________

I study in ____________________

Each one of us is special!

We are all the same, yet different in many ways.

No two people have the same fingerprints.

I like to play __________, but my friend likes to play __________.

I like to eat __________, but my friend likes to eat __________.

Recite the poem.

I am unique, I am me.
You may try, but you can never be me!
I have a face that is only mine.
I have qualities that make me fine!
I am special, one of a kind.
I think straight and speak my mind!

Let's Try

AI EL

Apply green poster paint to your right hand. Press your hand down onto the page and take your handprint. Decorate your handprint using dried flowers and leaves.

1 My Family: Sharing and Caring

Prior Knowledge

In the previous classes, I have learnt that

- Father, mother and children make a family.
- Some families are small, while some are big.
- The members of a family respect and help each other.

Learning Objectives

In this chapter, I will learn about:

- Family tree
- Types of families
- Having fun together

Let's Get Going

All of us belong to a family. Some families are small and some are big. Family members love, care for and protect one another. They share the housework. They also celebrate festivals together.

On a chart paper, create your own family tree. You can draw or paste pictures of your family members.

A nuclear family

TYPES OF FAMILIES

This is Seema's family.

She lives with her mother, father and brother.

They form a small family. Such families are also called **nuclear families**.

Real World

Some families are very small and consist of one parent and one or more children.

This is Nungsang's family.

Nungsang has ten members in his family.

He lives with his grandparents, parents, a sister, uncle, aunt and two cousins.

His father and his uncle are brothers.

The children of his uncle and aunts are his cousins.

They all live together in a big house.

Such big families are called **joint families**.

A joint family

It is important to be respectful towards each other, especially to the elder members of the family. We should spend time with them. Grandparents like to play and spend time with their grandchildren.

All members of a family should have at least one meal together. Every member of a family has a special duty at home.

Talk About

List three things that you do as a duty towards your family.

Let's Try

Write your name and surname.

________________ Name

________________ Surname

Having fun together

Different families have different ways of having fun together. They go out for picnics or to the circus or a zoo. Sometimes, they stay at home and play games together. Travelling with our family during vacations is also fun.

Your Task

Find out the meaning of the word 'twins'.

John and Lily are twins. It is their birthday today. They turned seven today. They are celebrating their birthday with family and friends.

Kids celebrating birthday

When there is a special **occasion** in the family, all the members and their friends get together to celebrate.

Family members support each other during happy and difficult times.

How do you spend time with your family?

My Dictionary

occasion: an important event or celebration

Knowledge Check

Write T for true or F for false.

1. There are more than five members in a small family. ☐
2. Parents with their children make a nuclear family. ☐
3. Joint families have grandparents, uncles and aunts. ☐
4. Family members should not sit together at mealtimes. ☐

Concept Map

Family

Nuclear family
has
Father, mother, child/children

Joint family
has
Grandparents, parents, uncle, aunt, cousins

Family members share responsibilities and take care of one another. They have fun together by going out and spending time together.

Summary

a. In this chapter, I have learnt that

- There are small and big families.
- Family members share responsibilities and take care of one another.
- Family members have fun by going out and spending time together.

b. I can do the following:

- Spend time with my grandparents
- Remember everyone's birthdays and wish them
- Help my family members whenever they need it

Practice ZONE

A. Write T for true or F for false.

1. Ravi lives with his mother and father. His family is small. ☐
2. In a family, only women do the housework. ☐
3. Twins share their birthday. ☐
4. When parents, grandparents, uncles, aunts and cousins live together, it is called a nuclear family. ☐

B. Fill in the blanks using the words given in the box.

support   big   love

1. Family members ________________, care for and protect each other.
2. Karan has eight family members in his family. It is a ________________ family.
3. Family members ________________ each other during happy and difficult times.

C. Give reasons for each of these.

1. We should spend time with our grandparents.

____

2. Special occasions bring in happy times.

____

D. Answer these questions in brief.

1. What is a joint family?

____

2. Write two fun activities that a family can do together.

____

E. Picture Talk

Identify the family members given in the picture.

F. Out of the box!

It is festival time and all your family members have gathered together for a feast. How will you show your respect towards them?

____

____

Skills Enrichment ZONE

A. 21 CS Life Skills | HQ Understanding Values in Relationships | 4 QUALITY EDUCATION

Alka's grandparents are coming over to spend winter holidays with them. Make a list of things that Alka can do to help her parents prepare for her grandparents' visit. Also, write the different things that she can do to make her grandparents feel comfortable and enjoy their stay.

B. 21 CS Information Literacy | CC Integration with English

Paste a picture of your family on a sheet or a chart paper. Write the names of your family members in alphabetical order. Use direction words, such as *to my left* or *right, in front of, behind, in between*, etc., to describe who is who in the picture.

C. 21 CS Creativity and Innovation, Life Skills | AI | HQ Understanding Values in Relationships

It is important to remember and wish all your family members on their birthdays. Make a list of your family members and write their birthdays in your notebook. Do not forget to make a birthday card for them beforehand.

2 My School

Prior Knowledge

In the previous classes, I have learnt that

- We go to school to learn, to play and to make friends.
- A school has different sections and different people to take care of us.
- We must follow rules in school.

Learning Objectives

In this chapter, I will learn about:

- Types of schools
- Things we learn in school
- Keeping the school clean

Let's Get Going

Fill in the blanks.

The name of my school is ______________________.

My principal's name is ______________________.

My class teacher's name is ______________________.

I go to school by ______________________.

I go to school wearing a ______________________.

My favourite subject in school is

______________________.

Names of some of my school friends are

____

____

Three things that I enjoy doing in school are

1. ____
2. ____
3. ____

TYPES OF SCHOOLS

Rosy is four years old. She goes to a **kindergarten school**. At school, she learns how to play with other children. She learns different rhymes and songs and about the things around her. Kindergarten school is for very young children.

When Rosy turns six years old, she will go to a **primary school**. When she grows older, she will go to a **high school**. After that, she will go to a **college**.

Knowledge Check

What kind of school do you think they go to?

1. Reena is three years old. She goes to a __________________ school.
2. Ali is fourteen years old. He goes to a __________________ school.
3. Ron is nine years old. He goes to a __________________ school.
4. Anu is nineteen years old. She goes to a __________________.

THINGS WE LEARN IN SCHOOL

Children learn different subjects in school. At home, we speak in our mother tongue. In school, we learn to read and write other languages. We study mathematics, environmental studies, and art and craft. We learn more about the world from stories of the past. We also play games and enjoy sports at school.

An important thing that we learn at school is how to be good and kind and behave in the right manner. We also learn to think and solve problems. School helps us make friends and we learn to get along with others.

Here are some other values that we learn in school.

- We learn to listen when others speak.
- We learn to wait for our turn at the playground.
- We learn to be caring, polite and respectful.
- We learn to share things with our friends.

KEEPING THE SCHOOL CLEAN

It is the duty of all children to keep their school clean.

Write three ways by which you can keep your school clean.

1. ______________________________

2. ______________________________

3. ______________________________

Concept Map

Types of School

- Kindergarten
  - For very small children
- Primary
  - For small children
- High
  - For older children

In school, we learn:

- to read and write different languages
- different subjects
- to be good, kind and behave in the right manner
- to think and to solve problems
- to make friends and to share things with them

Summary

a. In this chapter, I have learnt that

- We go to school to learn and play with our friends.
- There are different schools to which we go as we grow older.
- We study different subjects in school.
- We learn different values in school.

b. I can do the following:

- Learn different subjects in school
- Learn how to sing, dance and play sports in school
- Obey my teacher and help my friends
- Keep my school clean

Practice ZONE

A. Write T for true or F for false.

1. Kindergarten school is meant for very young children. ☐
2. We learn how to solve problems in school. ☐
3. After primary school, a boy or a girl goes to college. ☐
4. Schools usually have a zoo. ☐

B. Fill in the blanks using the words given in the box.

science	listen	primary

1. Rita is seven years old. She goes to a ______________ school.
2. ______________ teaches us about plants, animals, universe and how things work around us.
3. In school, we learn to ______________ when others speak.

C. Give reasons for each of these.

1. It is important for us to go to school.

____

2. We should not litter our school.

____

D. Answer these questions in brief.

1. Why do children go to school?

____

2. Name the different schools a child goes to in his life as a student.

____

3. Name three subjects you learn in your school.

____

E. Out of the box!

The Taj Mahal is in Agra, Uttar Pradesh. Which subject teaches us about the locations of various monuments and places?

____

____

F. Picture Talk

What do you think the teacher is teaching in the classroom?

Skills Enrichment ZONE

A. 21 CS Communication

Make a list of the things you do in school. Keep a record for a week and then discuss it with your friends and teacher in class.

B. 21 CS Communication

4 QUALITY EDUCATION

Look at your school diary and write down the address of your school. The address shows the exact location of your school. Do not forget to mention the name of your city or town or village.

C. 21 CS Critical Thinking, Life Skills HQ Understanding Values in Relationships

Your friend forgot to bring lunch. How will you help him or her?

Worksheet 1

STEAM CHALLENGE

You are going to a new class. Design a school bag with pockets for storing different things you need to carry such as your water bottle, tiffin box, books and pencil box.

What is the challenge?

What supplies do you need?

IDEA 1

IDEA 2

What worked or did not work for you?

How can you improve it?

3 My Body: Bones and Muscles

Prior Knowledge

In the previous classes, I have learnt that

- Our body has different parts.
- Sense organs help us to feel the world around us.
- We should take care of our body.

Learning Objectives

In this chapter, I will learn about:

- Bones and muscles
- Healthy bones and muscles

Let's Get Going

Follow the words of the song and do the actions.

Stand up straight with your feet apart.
Spread your arms and get, set, start!
Jump up high and raise your hand.
Slowly bend down and then up you stand!
Clap your hands and turn around.
Snap your fingers and tap your feet on the ground!
Jog on the spot and count till ten.
Once you stop, you do it again!
Show your tongue, squeeze your nose,
Nod your head and smile like a rose!
You can stop now and take some rest.
Exercise daily and be the fittest!

BONES AND MUSCLES

Press your left arm with your right hand. You will feel that some parts are hard and some are soft. Now, slowly feel the different parts of your body to identify the hard and soft parts. The hard parts are your **bones**, while the soft parts are your **muscles**. The bones and muscles in our body are covered with the skin.

Bones

Do you know we all have a skeleton inside our body? The bones in our body together form the skeleton.

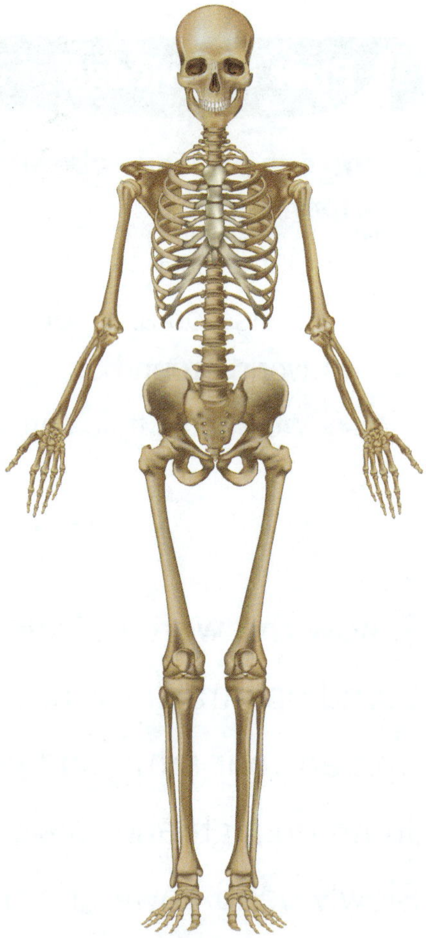

Skeleton

A new born baby has as many as 300 bones. Some of these bones join together as the baby grows. An adult human being has 206 bones.

The bones help us in many ways.

- They give shape to our body.
- They give support to our body.
- They protect all the organs inside our body.

Doctor showing X-ray picture

Sometimes during an accident we may break our bones. Doctors take an X-ray to check if there is any problem with our bones. An X-ray is a picture of the bones of our body.

Talk About

Have you ever seen an X-ray report? If yes, which part of the body was that?

Real World

Femur or thigh bone is the longest and the strongest bone in our body. The smallest bone is stapes or stirrup that is found inside our ears.

Joints

A joint is a place where two bones meet. Touch your elbow and feel the joint. They are like the **hinges** of a door. Because of the joints we can bend the different parts of our body. Joints help us move, bend or twist.

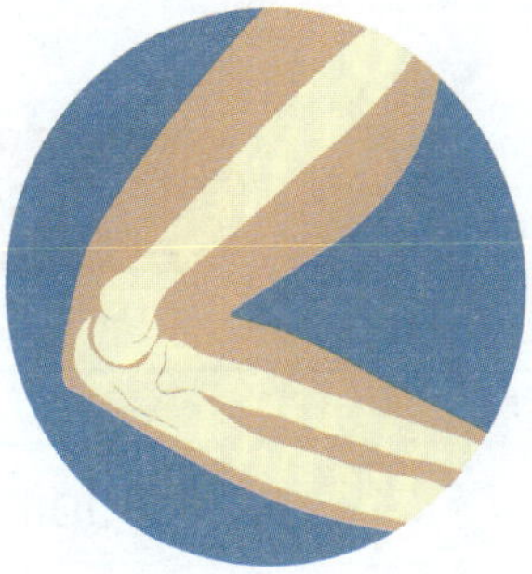

Elbow joint

My Dictionary

hinge: a joint on which a door or gate moves freely as it opens or closes

posture: the way you hold your body

Feel the joints in your finger. You can bend your fingers because of these joints. These joints help us hold pencil and write.

Your Task

Try picking up a glass or writing on a paper without bending your fingers.

Muscles

The soft parts in our body that lie below the skin are called **muscles**. Muscles are attached to the bones and together they help us move. There are more than 600 muscles in our body. Because of the muscles we can sit, walk, jump, write, eat and do other actions. They also help us maintain a good **posture**.

Knowledge Check

Match the following.

1. Joint	a. Hard parts in our body
2. Muscles	b. Where two bones meet
3. Bones	c. Soft parts in our body

HEALTHY BONES AND MUSCLES

It is important to eat the right food and exercise regularly to make our bones and muscles strong. Cycling, jogging and swimming are some exercises that you can do to stay fit.

To make our bones strong, we must include milk, curd, banana and spinach in our diet.

Cycling

Jogging

Swimming

Concept Map

My Body

is made up of

Bones

- The bones are the hard parts in our body that form the skeleton.
- An adult has 206 bones.
- Bones give shape and support to our body and protect all the organs inside our body.

Joints

- A joint is a place where two bones meet.
- A joint helps us to move, bend, twist and turn.

Muscles

- Muscles are the soft parts in our body that lie under the skin.
- Muscles help us move and maintain good posture.

Summary

a. In this chapter, I have learnt that

- The hard parts in our body are called bones and the soft parts are called muscles.
- The bones form a framework in our body called the skeleton.
- Bones and muscles together help us move.

b. I can do the following:

- Feel the bones in my body
- Exercise to make my bones and muscles strong

Practice ZONE

A. Name the following.

1. They are attached to the bones ____________
2. Place where two bones meet ____________
3. The framework of bones ____________
4. The longest bone in our body ____________

B. Write T for true or F for false.

1. An adult has more bones than a baby. ☐
2. Muscles give shape to our body. ☐
3. There are more than 600 bones in our body. ☐
4. Bones and muscles together help us move. ☐

C. Give reasons for each of these.

1. Daniel fell and hurt his leg. The doctor asked him to take an X-ray.

   ____
2. We can bend our knees.

   ____
3. We must include milk, curd, banana and spinach in our diet.

   ____

D. Answer these questions in brief.

1. Write any one use of bones in our body.

   ____
2. What is an X-ray?

   ____
3. What should you do to make your bones and muscles strong?

   ____

E. Picture Talk

Do you know that most animals have a skeleton inside them just like us. Match the following animals to their skeletons.

1. Crocodile

a. 

2. Frog

b. 

3. Giraffe

c. 

F. Out of the box!

Some of us do not maintain the right posture while walking, sitting or standing. We slouch or bend forward. How do you think it will affect our body?

____

____

Skills Enrichment ZONE

A. 21 CS Creativity and Innovation AI

Use toothpicks to create the given skeleton. You may draw the head with a pencil.

B. 21 CS Critical Thinking, Life skills

Your friend has broken his arm in the school playground. How can you help him?

3 GOOD HEALTH AND WELL-BEING

4 Food That Keeps Me Healthy

Prior Knowledge

In the previous classes, I have learnt that

- All living things need food to live.
- We need food to grow and stay healthy.
- We should eat healthy food and avoid junk food.

Learning Objectives

In this chapter, I will learn about:

- Importance of food
- Sources of food
- Kinds of food
- Raw and cooked food
- Dining etiquette

Let's Get Going

You are going out for a picnic. Fill up the basket by drawing the food items of your choice.

IMPORTANCE OF FOOD

Food gives us energy to work and play. It helps us stay active and grow. Food also keeps us healthy. What do you think will happen if a baby does not eat proper food?

Talk About

How do you feel when you are hungry? What do you do when you are hungry? How do you feel after that?

SOURCES OF FOOD

Food comes from both plants and animals. We eat different parts of plants as food.

Seeds such as pea, corn and bean

Roots such as carrot and radish

Leaves such as spinach and mint

Flowers such as cauliflower and broccoli

Stems such as celery and sugarcane

Here are some food items we get from animals.

Eggs

Chicken

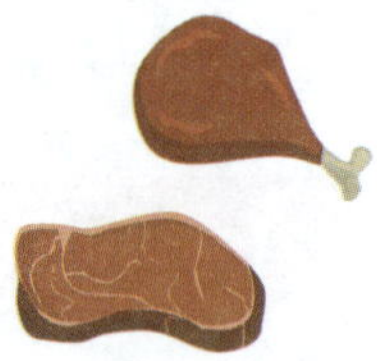
Mutton

Fish

KINDS OF FOOD

We need different foods in the correct quantity to stay healthy. Food can be classified into the following groups.

- Energy-giving food
- Body-building food
- Protective food

My Dictionary

labourer: a person who does hard physical work

Energy-giving food

The food that gives us energy to work and play is called **energy-giving food**. People who do a lot of physical activities such as sportsmen, **labourers** and growing children need a lot of energy-giving food.

Bread, pasta, potatoes, dosas, rice, rotis, oil and butter are some examples of energy-giving food.

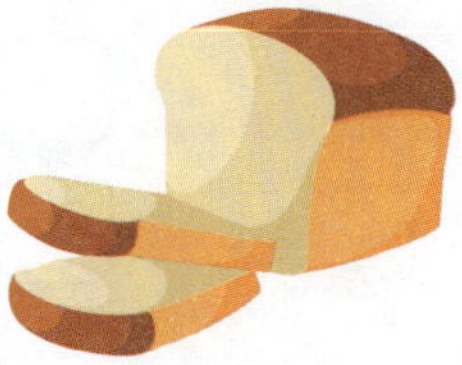
Bread

Pasta

Rice

Oil

Body-building food

The food that helps our body grow big and strong is called **body-building food**. This food makes our bones and muscles strong. Milk, fish, eggs, chicken, soya, curd and dal are the examples of body-building food.

Milk

Fish

Eggs

Dal

Protective food

The food that protects us from germs and diseases is called **protective food.** It keeps us healthy and fit. Fruits and vegetables are protective food.

Fruits and vegetables

WATER

Along with food, it is important that we drink plenty of water. We must drink at least eight glasses of water every day.

Talk About

What do you think will happen if you eat only rice?

HEALTHY EATING

We must eat all kinds of food and drink enough water. We must not overeat, otherwise we might fall sick. Eating too much junk food is not good for our health.

Your Task

Find out another English name for capsicum and brinjal.

Knowledge Check

Write T for true or F for false.

1. Our parents do not need body-building food. ☐
2. We should eat all kinds of food. ☐
3. Energy-giving food helps us grow. ☐
4. Junk food is good for us. ☐

RAW AND COOKED FOOD

Some food items can be eaten raw, while some needs to be cooked. We cook food to make it soft, tasty and germ-free.

Food items such as banana, apple, grapes can be eaten raw. Food items such as rice and wheat can be eaten only when cooked. Food items such as carrot, spinach and tomatoes can be eaten raw or cooked.

DINING ETIQUETTE

You should always follow table manners while eating, whether at home or at a restaurant.

- Wash your hands before eating.
- Place the napkin on your lap.
- Do not play with your **cutlery**.
- Hold the fork in your left hand and the knife or the spoon in your right hand.
- Wait for everyone to be served before you start eating.
- Always say 'please' when you want something. Say 'thank you' on being served.
- Do not chew with your mouth open.
- Do not talk with food in your mouth.

Family having dinner

My Dictionary

cutlery: spoon, knives and forks used while eating food

Concept Map

Food

- **Sources of Food**
  - Plants
  - Animals
- **Importance of Food**
  - Gives us energy to work and play
  - Keeps us healthy
- **Types of Food**
  - **Energy-giving Food**: Gives us energy to work and play
    - examples: Bread, rice, pasta
  - **Body-building Food**: Helps us grow big and strong
    - examples: Milk, fish, chicken, curd, dal
  - **Protective Food**: Keeps us healthy and fit and protects us from germs and diseases
    - examples: Fruits and vegetables

Summary

a. In this chapter, I have learnt that

- Food gives us energy, helps us grow and keeps us healthy.
- We get food from plants and animals.
- There are three groups of food: energy-giving food, body-building food and protective food.
- Food can be eaten raw or it can be cooked.
- We must follow dining etiquette.

b. I can do the following:

- Eat healthy food from all groups
- Avoid eating junk food
- Follow table manners

Practice ZONE

A. Choose the correct option.

1. Which of the following is not a food from a plant source?
   a. Beans b. Milk c. Cabbage
2. Which of the following cannot be eaten raw?
   a. Cucumber b. Tomato c. Potato
3. Which of the following is an energy-giving food?
   a. Ghee b. Grapes c. Curd

B. Write T for true or F for false.

1. Food helps us stay active. ☐
2. Fruits and vegetables are body-building food. ☐
3. We should not chew with our mouth open. ☐
4. All food items can be eaten raw. ☐

C. Give reasons for each of these.

1. Sunil likes to have pasta for dinner every day. His mother thinks it is not good for him.
   ____
2. Jacob has fallen sick. The doctor has advised him to eat fruits and vegetables.
   ____
3. We need to cook some of the food items.
   ____

D. Answer these questions in brief.

1. Why do we need food?
   ____
2. Give an example for each of the following parts of the plant that we eat.
   - Leaf ____________
   - Root ____________
   - Seed ____________
   - Flower ____________
3. What kind of food does a sportsperson need and why?
   ____

E. Name a food item of each of the following colour.

1. Green ____________ 2. Red ____________
3. Yellow ____________ 4. Orange ____________

F. Picture Talk

Identify the following food groups as energy-giving, protective and junk food.

1. 
____

2. 
____

3. 
____

G. Out of the box!

Breakfast is the most important meal of the day. It should include a lot of energy-giving food. Why?

____

____

Skills Enrichment ZONE

A. 21 CS Collaboration, Communication HQ Knowing My Needs

3 GOOD HEALTH AND WELL-BEING

Form a group with your four classmates. Think and discuss a day's menu that is healthy and includes food from all the groups. Write it on a paper and put it up on the softboard.

B. 21 CS Creativity and Innovation AI HQ Knowing My Needs

Draw two healthy and two unhealthy food items in your notebook. Name them.

C. 21 CS Critical Thinking, Life Skills

4 QUALITY EDUCATION

Reena goes to her friend's house for her birthday and does not like the food that is served on the table. What should she do?

1. Tell her friend that she has a stomach ache. ☐
2. Eat a little. ☐
3. Take her plate and throw the food in the bin. ☐

Safety Rules

Let us revise the safety rules as they keep us safe and prevent accidents.

At Home

- Do not play with sharp objects such as knives and needles.
- Do not leave toilet floor wet.
- Do not play with electric wires or plug points.
- Do not touch electric gadgets with wet hands.
- Do not play with fire or matchsticks.

On the Road

- Walk on the footpath.
- Use the zebra crossing.
- Follow the traffic lights.
- While walking on the road, walk on the right side of the road so that you can see the traffic coming from the front.

At School

- Follow school rules.
- Do not run down the corridor.
- Do not play with pointed pencils and scissors.
- Listen carefully to your teachers' instructions and follow them.

At the Playground

- Wait for your turn on the rides and swings.
- Do not play rough games.
- Do not stand in front of a moving swing.
- Do not push your friends.

In the Bus

- Stand in a queue while waiting for a bus.
- Do not stand in a moving bus.
- Do not put your head or hands out of the window.
- Do not disturb the driver by shouting or talking to him.

Worksheet 2

STEAM CHALLENGE

Your friends in your class have different heights. How would you measure their heights?

What is the challenge?

What supplies do you need?

1

2

What worked or did not work for you?

How can you improve it?

5 Occupations

Prior Knowledge

In the previous classes, I have learnt that

- Many people help us and make our lives easier and better.
- We must respect and thank people who make our lives comfortable.

Learning Objectives

In this chapter, I will learn about:

- Occupation
- Different occupations
- Respecting people who help us

Let's Get Going

Look at the pictures and unscramble the letters to find the occupations of people who help us.

OLTAIR ____________

EHCRATE ____________

ANLCERE ____________

RTDOOC ____________

INMFARE ____________

DIFFERENT OCCUPATIONS

People do different jobs. A job or work that people do for a living is called their **occupation**.

Remember

One who writes songs is called a lyricist.

Talk About

What would happen if there were no garbage collectors?

We should respect the people of all occupations. We should be kind and polite to them. We should never ill-treat them. We must thank everyone who makes our lives comfortable.

Knowledge Check

Name the following.

1. A person who sells fish ______________
2. A person who makes and repairs things made of iron ______________
3. A person who sells medicines ______________
4. A person who makes paintings ______________
5. A person who repairs vehicles ______________

Concept Map

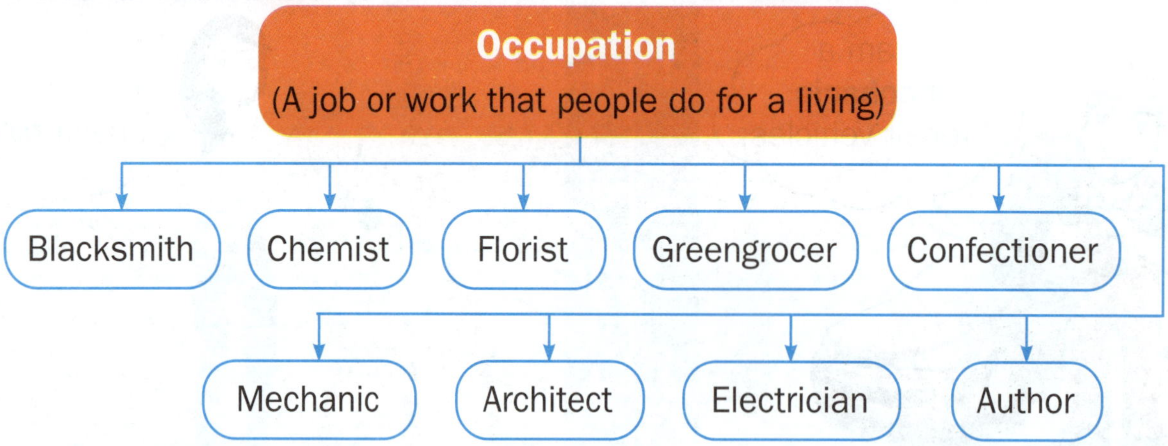

Summary

a. In this chapter, I have learnt that

- People do different jobs to earn money.
- Some people such as chemist, greengrocer, blacksmith, fishmonger, electrician, mechanic, florist and confectioner are found in our neighbourhood.
- We should respect the people of all occupations.

b. I can do the following:

- Help my mother buy vegetables and fruits from the greengrocer
- Respect people who make our lives comfortable

Practice ZONE

A. Write T for true or F for false.

1. A confectioner sells medicines. ☐
2. An electrician lays electric wires and fittings. ☐
3. A mechanic makes and repairs things made of iron. ☐
4. An architect designs buildings. ☐

B. Fill in the blanks using the words given in the box.

blacksmith	musician	greengrocer	mechanic

1. A ________________ plays musical instruments.
2. A ________________ repairs a broken car.
3. My mother went to a ________________ to buy vegetables.
4. Rajiv needs to repair his iron chain, he will go to ________________ .

C. Give reasons for each of these.

1. We should respect the people of all occupations.

   ____

2. A doctor also needs holidays.

   ____

D. Answer these questions in brief.

1. What is an occupation?

   ____

2. Name four people who have shops in your neighbourhood market.

   ____

3. Who is a confectioner?

   ____

E. Picture Talk

Identify and write the names of the people who help us.

____________ ____________ ____________ ____________

F. Out of the box!

Mr Raju is going to build a new home. Name the people he will need to help him build his house.

____

____

Skills Enrichment ZONE

A. 21 CS Information Literacy | AI | HQ Living in an Interconnected Society

8 DECENT WORK AND ECONOMIC GROWTH

Find out the names of five jobs that people do other than those described in the book. What are they called? Collect their pictures and paste them in your exercise book. Do not forget to label them neatly.

B. 21 CS Communication

Conduct an interview of a shopkeeper or storekeeper in your neighbourhood market. Read out the interview in class. Your teacher can help you with the interview questions.

C. 21 CS Life Skills | AI | HQ Cooperation and Collaborative Living

10 REDUCED INEQUALITIES

People do different jobs to earn money and support themselves and their families. We should respect and value every job. Name the people who help in your daily life from morning till night. How would your life be if they were not around? Make a 'Thank You' card and give it to a person who you think has made your life easier.

6 Celebrating Together

Prior Knowledge

In the previous classes, I have learnt that

- We celebrate special days with our family and friends.
- India is a land of festivals.
- There are two types of festivals—religious festivals and national festivals.

Learning Objectives

In this chapter, I will learn about:

- Types of festivals
- Celebrating festivals

Let's Get Going

Look at the pictures and write the names of the festivals they represent.

_______________ _______________

_______________ _______________

TYPES OF FESTIVALS

Festivals bring joy, happiness and unity. People in India celebrate different festivals throughout the year. We celebrate festivals with people living in the same building or **locality** by dancing, singing and eating together.

We have learnt about some of the festivals in Class 1. Let us learn more about them.

We celebrate three types of festivals in India.

- Religious festivals
- Harvest festivals
- National festivals

My Dictionary

locality: the area we live in

Religious festivals

In India, different religions are followed. People belonging to different religions celebrate various festivals. These are called religious festivals. These festivals are celebrated throughout the country by every one.

Let us learn about some of these religious festivals.

Dussehra is a festival that is celebrated to mark the victory of Lord Rama over Ravana. People celebrate the victory of good over evil. People go to various parks to see 'Ram Lila', which is a drama showing the life of Lord Rama.

Diwali is a festival of lights. It is celebrated twenty days after Dussehra. On this day, Lord Rama along with his wife Sita and brother Lakshman returned home to Ayodhya after killing Ravana. People clean and decorate their homes and exchange sweets.

Eid is a festival that marks the end of the month of fasting called Ramazan or Ramadan. People pray in mosques and wish each other 'Eid Mubarak'. They cook a special sweet dish called *sewaiyan*.

Gurpurab is the celebration of the birth anniversary of Guru Nanak Dev. A kitchen called *langar* is set up where free food is served to all visitors.

Christmas is celebrated on 25th December every year. People go to church and pray. Families enjoy meals together and exchange gifts. People eat and distribute cakes on this day.

Holi is the festival of colours that marks the arrival of spring. A night before Holi, a bonfire is lit and people go around it singing songs. The next day, people play with colours and distribute sweets.

Harvest festivals

Harvest is the time when crops are ready to be cut. Different festivals related to harvest time are celebrated in different parts of India. These are called harvest festivals.

Let us learn about some harvest festivals.

Onam is a harvest festival celebrated in Kerala. People make rangolis with flowers in their houses. Snake boat race is conducted during the festival of Onam.

Baisakhi is the harvest festival of Punjab. It is celebrated in the month of April. People perform bhangra to celebrate this festival.

Gudi Padwa is the harvest festival of Maharashtra. People welcome the new year by placing a long decorated stick called *Gudi* in front of their houses.

Bihu is the biggest harvest festival of Assam. People dance and sing Bihu songs on this day. People exchange traditional sweets and greetings at this time.

Pongal is a harvest festival of Tamil Nadu. A special dish called Pongal rice is cooked with milk and jaggery (*gur*).

Knowledge Check

Write T for true or F for false.

1. Holi is celebrated twenty days after Dussehra. ☐
2. On Eid, a special dish called *sewaiyan* is made. ☐
3. Onam is the harvest festival of Tamil Nadu. ☐
4. Baisakhi is celebrated in April. ☐

National festivals

The celebration of national festivals makes us proud and happy to be Indians. Republic Day, Independence Day and Gandhi Jayanti are celebrated as national festivals in our country.

Republic Day parade

Republic Day is celebrated on 26th January every year. It was on this day that the Rule Book of India was given to its people. To celebrate the occasion, a colourful parade is held on Rajpath in New Delhi. The President of India takes the salute at the parade.

Unfurling of Indian flag on Independence Day

Independence Day is celebrated on 15th August every year. This was the day when India got independence from the British rule in the year 1947. On this day, the Prime Minister of India **unfurls** the national flag and gives a speech to the country from the Red Fort, Delhi.

My Dictionary

unfurls: spreads out or unfolds

Talk About

How are religious festivals, harvest festivals and national festivals different from each other?

Gandhi Jayanti is the birth anniversary of the 'Father of the Nation', Mahatma Gandhi. It is celebrated on 2nd October every year.

Mahatma Gandhi

Concept Map

Festivals

types:

- **Religious festivals** — examples:
  - Dussehra
  - Diwali
  - Eid
  - Gurpurab
  - Christmas
  - Holi
- **Harvest festivals** — examples:
  - Onam
  - Baisakhi
  - Gudi Padwa
  - Bihu
  - Pongal
- **National festivals** — examples:
  - Republic Day
  - Independence Day
  - Gandhi Jayanti

Summary

a. In this chapter, I have learnt that

- Festivals bring joy, happiness and unity.
- There are three kinds of festivals in India: religious, harvest and national.
- Holi, Diwali, Dussehra, Gurpurab, Eid and Christmas are the religious festivals.
- Onam, Baisakhi, Gudi Padwa, Bihu and Pongal are the harvest festivals.
- Independence Day, Republic Day and Gandhi Jayanti are the national festivals.

b. I can do the following:

- Help my mother decorate the house during festivals
- Differentiate between religious and national festivals
- Show respect to my country by standing in attention position on hearing the national anthem

Practice ZONE

A. Match the following.

1. Diwali	a. *Sewaiyan*
2. Christmas	b. Langar
3. Gurpurab	c. Sweet rice dish
4. Eid	d. Christmas cake
5. Pongal	e. Festival of lights

B. Fill in the blanks using the words given in the box.

President	Prime Minister	Onam	Bihu	Eid

1. ______________ is a harvest festival of Assam.
2. The harvest festival of Kerala is called ______________.
3. ______________ is a festival that comes after the month of Ramadan.
4. On Republic Day, the ______________ of India takes the salute at the parade.
5. On Independence Day, the ______________ of India addresses the nation.

C. Give reasons for each of these.

1. We should stand in attention when the national anthem is being played.

   ____
2. People celebrate harvest festivals.

   ____
3. Diwali is called the festival of lights.

   ____

D. Answer these questions in brief.

1. When is Diwali celebrated?

   ____
2. Name any two harvest festivals celebrated in India.

   ____
3. Where is the Republic Day parade held?

   ____

E. Picture Talk

In which festival do we decorate the given tree? Colour and decorate this tree.

F. Out of the box!

Raman wants to celebrate a 'Green Diwali' with his family and friends this year. Suggest ways to help him celebrate it.

____

____

Skills Enrichment ZONE

A. 21 CS Communication IF HQ Living in an Interconnected Society

In this chapter, you have learnt about the different festivals celebrated in our country. Find out about two more Indian festivals and how they are celebrated.

B. 21 CS Critical Thinking, Information Literacy CC Integration with English

Arrange these festivals in alphabetical order.

Diwali Onam Eid Christmas Gurpurab Baisakhi
Gudi Padwa Pongal Republic Day Gandhi Jayanti

____

____

C. 21 CS Critical Thinking, Creativity and Innovation AI HQ Coexisting with Nature IF

13 CLIMATE ACTION

Diwali is the time for us to celebrate. But it can be harmful too!
Make a poster to tell people

- not to dirty the air,
- not to disturb animals or sick people and
- to share and care.

Worksheet 3

STEAM CHALLENGE

Make a *Rangoli* for decorating your house using flower petals or coloured powder or coloured paper.

What is the challenge?

What supplies do you need?

1

2

What worked or did not work for you?

How can you improve it?

7 Plants

Prior Knowledge

In the previous classes, I have learnt that

- Plants have different shapes and sizes.
- Different plants grow in different places.
- Plants need air, water, sunlight and soil to grow.
- Plants give shade, clean air and food.

Learning Objectives

In this chapter, I will learn about:

- Different types of plants
- Uses of plants
- What plants need to grow

Let's Get Going

Look at the rose plant. Do you think it will grow as big as the neem tree?

Rose plant

Neem tree

________ (Yes/No), it ________ (will/will not) grow as big as the neem tree.

DIFFERENT TYPES OF PLANTS

There are different types of plants. Let us learn about them.

Trees

Some plants grow big and strong. They have a thick stem called **trunk** and lots of branches. The branches of trees have leaves, flowers and fruits. Trees live for many years. They grow in different places.

Mango tree

Banyan tree

Shrubs

Shrubs are small bushes with hard and thin stems. They do not grow as big as trees. They have many branches and live for many years. For example, *Hibiscus*.

Hibiscus

Herbs

Plants such as mint and coriander are seasonal plants that grow for a short time or for one season. Such plants are called **herbs**. They are very small and have thin green stems.

Mint

Climbers

Plants such as grapevine and money plant have weak stems; so, they cannot stand up straight on their own. Such plants are called **climbers**. Climbers need **support** to climb up.

Grapevine

Creepers

Plants such as the watermelon and pumpkin have very weak stems. They do not climb but creep on the ground. They are called **creepers**.

Pumpkin

Knowledge Check

Write T for true or F for false.

1. The *Hibiscus* plant is a herb. ☐
2. Climbers need support to climb up. ☐
3. Mango trees live for a short time. ☐
4. Grapevine is a creeper. ☐

My Dictionary

support: to give help

Remember

Small, tiny plants are called seedlings.

USES OF PLANTS

Plants are very useful to us. We must grow more plants and trees. Here are some of the uses of plants.

- They give us oxygen for breathing.
- Plants and trees are homes to many animals, birds and insects.
- We get tea, coffee, cocoa, jaggery and sugar from plants.

Cocoa plant → Cocoa beans → Chocolate

Sugarcane → Jaggery, Sugar

- Medicines are made from plants such as *Aloe vera*, *tulsi*, mint and garlic.
- Perfumes are made from flowers.

Perfume from rose flowers

- Rubber is obtained from rubber trees.

Rubber tree → Products made of rubber

- Wood from plants is used to make furniture.

Wood → Wooden chair

- Paper is obtained from bamboo plant.

Bamboo → Notebook

- **Fibres** such as jute and cotton are obtained from plants.

Jute plant → Jute bag; Cotton plant → Cotton dress

My Dictionary

fibres: thin thread-like material that are used to make cloth, bags, ropes, etc.

WHAT PLANTS NEED TO GROW

- Plants need water, sunlight, air and soil to grow.

- Plants need our care to grow and stay healthy.

Act Green

We should not destroy plants by plucking their leaves or flowers. We should protect the precious plants around us.

Concept Map

Types of Plants

- Trees → Big and strong → Mango, banyan
- Shrubs → Bushes with hard thin stems → *Tulsi, Hibiscus*
- Herbs → Seasonal small plants with thin green stems → Coriander
- Climbers → Weak stems that need support to grow → Money plant
- Creepers → Weak stems, creep on the ground → Pumpkin

Uses of Plants

plants provide

- Oxygen
- Home for living things
- Paper
- Food
- Fibres
- Wood
- Medicines
- Perfumes

Summary

a. In this chapter, I have learnt that

- Big plants with strong trunks are called trees.
- Shrubs have woody stems that are not as strong as trees.
- Herbs grow for one season and have green stems.

b. I can do the following:

- Recognize different plants
- Grow a plant and take care of it

Practice ZONE

A. Match the following.

1. Rose	a. Creeper
2. Neem	b. Climber
3. Mint	c. Tree
4. Watermelon	d. Herb
5. Grapes	e. Shrub

B. Fill in the blanks using the words given in the box.

shrubs	climbers	trunk	herbs

1. The thick stem of trees is called a ______________.
2. ______________ have very weak stems and they need support.
3. ______________ grow for a season.
4. ______________ are small bushes with hard stems.

C. Give reasons for each of these.

1. A grapevine needs support to grow.

   ____

2. Rohan put a plant in a cupboard. It died.

   ____

3. Cutting down trees affects birds and insects.

   ____

D. Answer these questions in brief.

1. What is the difference between a climber and a creeper?

   ____

2. What does a plant need to grow?

   ____

3. Name the plant from which paper is obtained.

   ____

E. Picture Talk

Look at the following pictures and name one item made from each of these.

Wood

Bamboo

Cotton plant

______________ ______________ ______________

F. Out of the box!

Why is watermelon a creeper and not a climber?

____

____

Skills Enrichment ZONE

A. 21 CS Creativity and Innovation | AI | HQ Happiness My Goal

Collect leaves of different shapes. Choose the leaves and arrange them to make a leaf elephant and paste it in your scrapbook.

B. 21 CS Critical Thinking, Life Skills | HQ Coexisting with Nature

Many people cut plants and trees to make space for building houses and offices. Do you think it is the right thing to do? Think of a way by which we can build a house without cutting plants and trees.

13 CLIMATE ACTION

C. 21 CS Life Skills | EL

Take some mustard seeds and some gram (*chana*) seeds. Plant them in two pots. Place the pots out in the open or on a windowsill. Water them regularly to keep the soil wet. Observe them daily and record your observations. Which one grows faster?

15 LIFE ON LAND

8 Animals

Prior Knowledge

In the previous classes, I have learnt that

- Animals live on land, trees and in water.
- Some animals are big and some are small.

Learning Objectives

In this chapter, I will learn about:

- What animals eat
- Where animals live
- Importance of animals

Let's Get Going

Look at the pictures carefully. Write W for wild animals and D for domestic animals.

WHAT ANIMALS EAT

Deer

Some animals such as giraffes, elephants, deer and hippopotamuses eat only plants.
They are called **plant-eating animals**.

Wild animals such as tigers, lions, crocodiles and leopards hunt and kill other animals for food. These animals eat the flesh of other animals and are called **flesh-eating animals**.

Some animals such as vultures and hyenas eat the flesh of dead animals.
They are called **scavengers**.

Animals such as bears and crows eat both plants and flesh of animals.

Lion

Bear

Hyena

Knowledge Check

Name the following.

1. An animal that eats the flesh of dead animals ____________
2. A plant-eating animal ____________
3. An animal that kills other animals for food ____________

WHERE ANIMALS LIVE

Wild animals such as tigers, lions, deers and zebras live on land. Some animals such as monkeys and birds live on trees. Some animals such as fish and whales live in water. Some animals such as crocodiles can live both on land and in water.

Real World

- Giraffe is the tallest animal in the world.
- No two zebras have the same stripes.

Some wild animals make homes for themselves.

Lions and tigers live in a den.

Bears live in a cave.

Rabbits live in a burrow.

Snakes live in a hole.

Birds live in a nest.

Bees live in a beehive.

Some animals live in human-made homes.

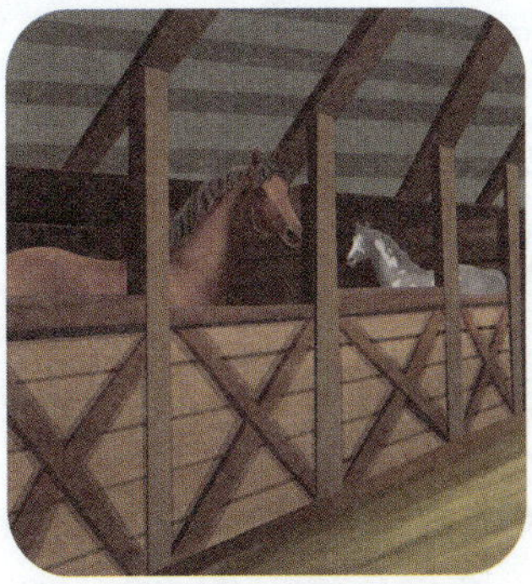

Horses are kept in a stable.

Cows are kept in a shed.

Hens are kept in a coop.

Dogs are kept in a kennel.

Sheep are kept in a pen.

Fish are kept in a fish bowl or an aquarium.

IMPORTANCE OF ANIMALS

Animals are useful to us. They give us many things such as milk, eggs, meat, honey, silk and wool. Animals such as horses, elephants, camels and oxen are used to carry heavy loads and people from one place to another.

Pets also help us in various ways. Dogs guard our house and cats chase the mice away.

Real World

We must feed our pets and domestic animals and look after them.

Your Task

- Find out the name of one more thing that we get from animals.
- Find out the meaning of milch cattle.

Concept Map

Animals

types

- Plant-eating
  - They eat only plants. Examples: Deer, giraffe
- Scavengers
  - They eat flesh of dead animals. Examples: Vulture, hyena
- Flesh-eating
  - They eat flesh of other animals. Examples: Tiger, lion

Summary

a. In this chapter, I have learnt that

- Animals are plant-eating or flesh-eating.
- Some animals such as bears eat both flesh and plants.
- Wild animals live on trees, in caves, dens, burrows, holes and hives.
- Animals give us milk, eggs, meat, honey, silk and wool.

b. I can do the following:

- Recognize wild and domestic animals
- Look after my pet

Practice ZONE

A. Fill in the blanks using the words given in the box.

dog	crow	deer	wild

1. A __________ eats grass.
2. Animals that live in forests are called __________ animals.
3. A __________ is a domestic animal.
4. A __________ eats both plants and flesh of other animals.

B. Write T for true or F for false.

1. A hyena is a plant-eating animal. ☐
2. Cows are kept in a shed. ☐
3. A bear lives in a cave. ☐
4. A zebra eats both plants and animals. ☐

C. Give reasons for each of these.

1. We cannot have giraffe as a pet.
____
2. Lion is not a scavenger.
____
3. Scavengers keep the jungle clean.
____

D. Answer these questions in brief.

1. What do cows, bulls and giraffes eat?
____
2. What do vultures eat?
____
3. Name some of the things that we get from animals.
____
4. Name two plant-eating animals.
____

E. Picture Talk

I am a cow. Write any four things that you would feed me.

____

____

____

____

F. Out of the box!

Why do you think that zebras in the US and India live in the zoo?

____

____

Skills Enrichment ZONE

A. 21 CS Creativity and Innovation | AI | HQ Coexisting with Nature

15 LIFE ON LAND

Draw animal's faces at the back of old cards and cut them out. Paste them on the front and back of a matchbox to make your animal stand. You can create as many animals as you like and put them together and have a matchbox zoo.

B. 21 CS Information Literacy | CC Integration with English

Complete the table.

Animals	Sounds	Homes	Babies
Lion	roars	den	cubs
Horse			
Cow			
Dog			

9 Birds and Insects

Prior Knowledge

In the previous classes, I have learnt that

- Birds have wings, feathers and beaks.
- Insects are very small in size with three pairs of legs.

Learning Objectives

In this chapter, I will learn about:

- How birds fly
- What birds eat
- Where birds live
- Insects

Let's Get Going

Look at the pictures and identify the birds using the word help.

Emu Penguin Parrot Hen Swan Crow Peacock Eagle

____

____

____

____

____

____

____

____

Talk about something special you know about each bird.

HOW BIRDS FLY

Birds are our feathered friends. They fly with the help of their wings and strong flight muscles. Their tails help them to change direction while flying.

Real World

Our national bird peacock is also called peafowl. The fan of its tail is called a train.

WHAT BIRDS EAT

Birds have beaks that help them eat. Different birds have different beaks to suit the way they eat their food. Some birds have sharp, pointed beaks, while others have blunt beaks.

My Dictionary

nectar: a sweet juice made by plants

Birds such as sparrows, hens and wrens eat seeds. Some birds such as hoopoe and woodpecker eat worms and insects. There are others such as heron and stork that eat flesh and fish. Some birds such as sunbird also drink **nectar** from flowers.

Hoopoe

Parrot

Duck

Seed-eating birds

Fish-eating bird

WHERE BIRDS LIVE

Have you seen birds carrying grass, twigs, dry leaves, paper or string in their beaks? They use these to make their nests.

The place where birds live with their young ones is called a **nest**. Birds build their nests at various places, such as trees, roofs of houses and even on the ground.

Parent bird feeding its young ones

Birds lay and hatch eggs in their nests. Parent birds take care of their young ones till they develop feathers and learn to fly.

Your Task

Find out what is a fledgling.

Some birds such as swans and ducks live on water. They have **webbed** feet that help them swim.

Some birds such as storks and cranes cannot swim but wade in water. They stand in water and catch fish for food.

My Dictionary

webbed: the toes are joined with skin

Webbed feet of swan

Stork

Knowledge Check

Fill in the blanks.

1. Birds fly with the help of ____________ and ____________.
2. Birds eat with their ____________.
3. Birds live with their young ones till they learn to ____________.
4. ____________ cannot swim but wade in water.

INSECTS

Insects are found in every part of the world. Insects have six legs and two antennae or feelers on their heads. The antennae help them sense their enemies. Insects usually have wings that help them fly.

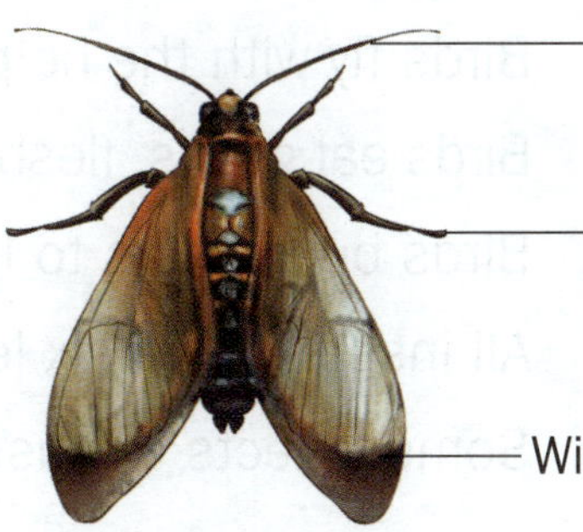

Parts of an insect

Some insects are useful to us. Honeybees provide us with honey. Ants are scavengers and butterflies make our surroundings beautiful. Some insects such as mosquitoes, cockroaches and houseflies spread diseases and are harmful.

Concept Map

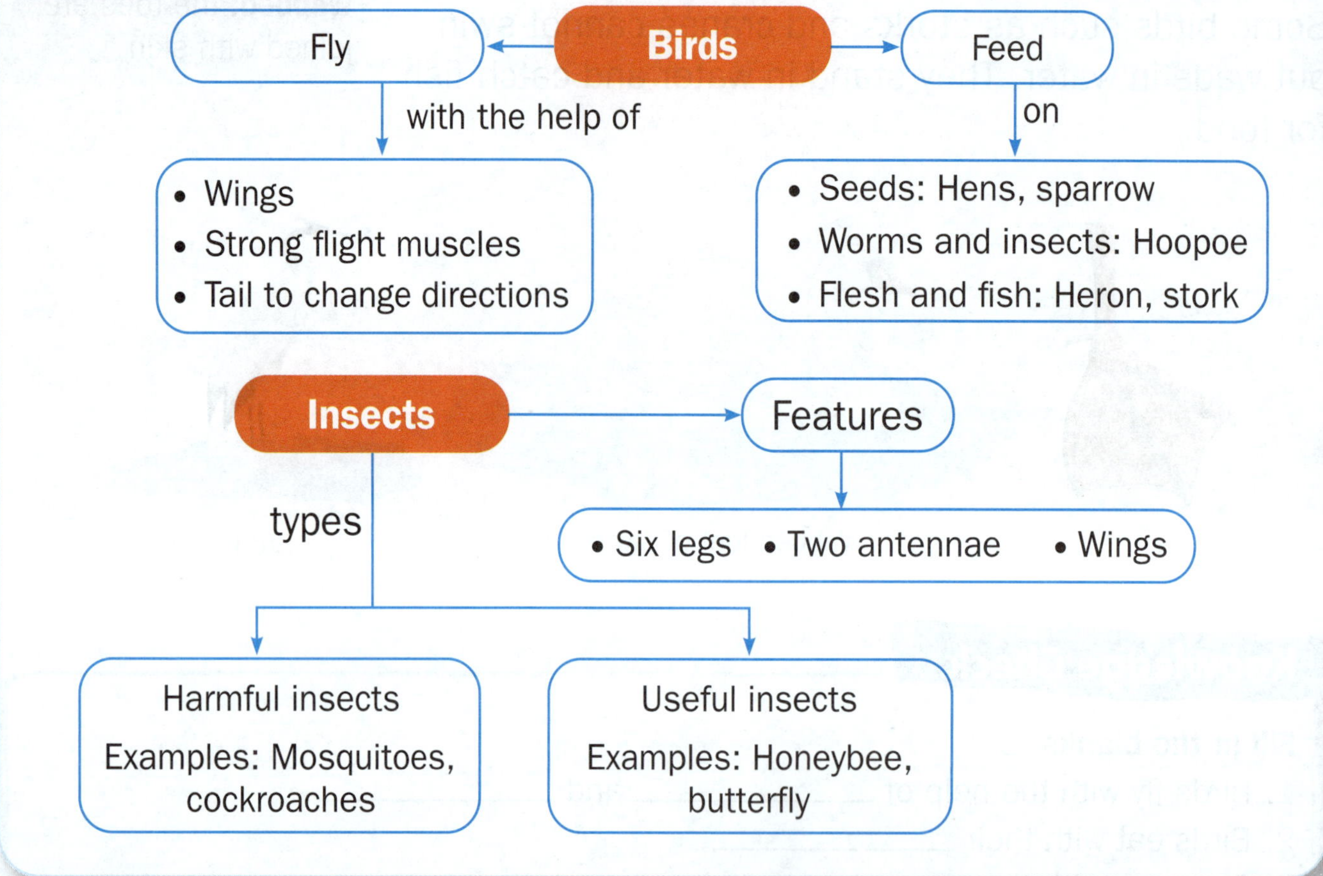

Summary

a. In this chapter, I have learnt that

- Birds fly with the help of wings, flight muscles and tail.
- Birds eat grains, flesh, fish, worms and insects and drink nectar.
- Birds build nests to lay eggs and take care of their young ones.
- All insects have six legs and two feelers. Some insects have wings.
- Some insects are useful while some are harmful.

b. I can do the following:

- Name the common birds
- Identify insects and classify them as useful and harmful

Practice ZONE

A. Write T for true or F for false.

1. Emus cannot fly.
2. Eagles eat fruits.
3. Wrens eat seeds.
4. A wading bird stands in water.
5. Honeybees provide us with honey.

B. Match the following.

1. Sunbird	a. Fish
2. Hoopoe	b. Grains
3. Sparrow	c. Nectar
4. Stork	d. Insects

C. Give reasons for each of these.

1. A bird is different from an insect.

___

2. Many houses put netting on the windows.

___

3. Not all insects are harmful to us.

___

D. Answer these questions in brief.

1. How do the antennae help an insect? Name two harmful insects.

___

2. What helps a bird change its direction while flying?

___

3. What helps a bird fly?

___

E. Picture Talk

Label the parts of a housefly.

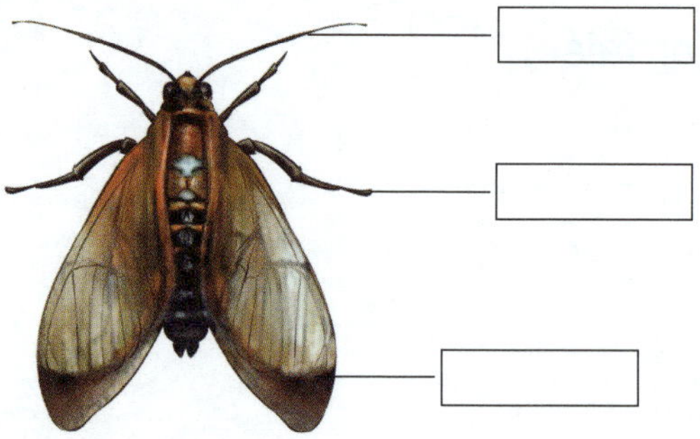

F. Out of the box!

1. What is common between an owl and a kiwi?

____

2. What is common between a penguin and an emu?

____

Skills Enrichment ZONE

A. 21 CS Creativity and Innovation | EL | HQ Living in an Interconnected Society

15 LIFE ON LAND

Make your own bird bath.

Take a small bowl and fill it with water. Put it out on the windowsill or in the garden outside your house.

Remember to change the water every day. Birds need water for drinking. They also need water to remove dust, loose feathers and other things from their body.

B. 21 CS Critical Thinking, Information Literacy | CC Integration with English

Think of the sounds birds make and fill in the blanks. One has been done for you.

Duck	Quacks	Chicken	________
Pigeon	________	Dove	________
Crow	________	Cuckoo	________
Parrot	________	Eagle	________

Worksheet 4

STEAM CHALLENGE

Make a model of a bird house using different recycled materials. Add different animals playing around the bird house. You can reuse small plastic balls and straws to make the animals.

What is the challenge?

What supplies do you need?

IDEA 1

IDEA 2

What worked or did not work for you?

How can you improve it?

10 Housing and Clothing

Prior Knowledge

In the previous classes, I have learnt that

- We live in a house to be safe.
- A house is made up of different materials.
- We wear clothes to cover our bodies.

Learning Objectives

In this chapter, I will learn about:

- Why we need a house
- Kinds of houses
- Keeping our homes clean
- Types of clothes
- Fibres
- Looking after our clothes

Let's Get Going

Draw and colour a picture of your house in the space provided.

WHY WE NEED HOUSES

A family lives together in a house. Our house keeps us safe and warm during the cold season, dry during the rains and cool during the hot season. Houses are made of different building materials. Some houses are strong, while some are not so strong.

In cities, most houses are made from building materials such as bricks, cement and steel. These are called ***pucca*** houses. A bungalow is an example of *pucca* house.

In villages, some houses are made from materials such as mud, bamboo, straw, ropes and sand. These are called ***kutcha*** houses. A hut is an example of *kutcha* house.

Pucca house

Kutcha house

KINDS OF HOUSES

There are mainly two kinds of houses: permanent and temporary.

Permanent houses

Permanent houses such as bungalows, cottages and apartments are very strong.

Bungalow

Cottage

Real World

Some houses in cities are in a row, joined by a common boundary wall. They are called row houses.

Remember

Very tall buildings in a city are called skyscrapers.

Temporary houses

Temporary houses such as tents, yurts, caravans and houseboats can be moved from place to place. People who keep moving from one place to another often build such houses.

Yurt is a type of traditional tent used in some areas.

A **caravan** is a house on wheels.

Tent is made of a strong cloth. It is used by campers.

A **houseboat** is a floating house made of wood.

HOUSES IN SPECIAL PLACES

In places with heavy rainfall and snowfall, houses have sloping roofs so that the rainwater and snow can easily slide down and not collect on the roof. Houses in rainy areas are built on stilts (wooden poles) to keep them safe from flooding water. A house made of snow is called an **igloo**. They are found in places that are covered with snow throughout the year.

Sloping roofs

Stilts

Igloo

KEEPING OUR HOMES CLEAN

It is very important to keep our houses clean.

All members of a family must help keep the home clean. We must throw waste and kitchen garbage in the bins. These bins must be cleaned and emptied every day. We should make sure that no water is collected in any dish because standing water can breed mosquitoes.

We all need to do our bit to keep our homes clean and free from germs. A clean home is a happy home.

Knowledge Check

Fill in the blanks.

1. Houses made from blocks of ice are called ________.
2. Houses are built on ________ to protect them from flooding water.
3. The houses made of bricks, cement and steel are called ________ houses.
4. A ________ is a floating house made of wood.

TYPES OF CLOTHES

Clothes protect our body from heat, rain and cold. We wear different clothes during different seasons.

During summer season, we wear light cotton clothes that keep our body cool.

Clothes for summer season

During rainy season, we wear raincoats and gumboots and carry an umbrella to keep ourselves dry. During winter season, we wear woollen clothes that protect us from cold and keep us warm.

Clothes for rainy season

Clothes for winter season

FIBRES

Clothes are made up of fibres. Fibres are thread-like materials that are woven together to make fabric. Fibres are either natural or artificial.

Natural fibres come from plants and animals. Cotton, jute, wool and silk are natural fibres.

Artificial fibres are human-made fibres. Examples of artificial fibres are rayon, nylon, terylene and polyester.

Cotton from cotton plants is used to make cotton clothes.

Wool from sheep is used to make woollen clothes.

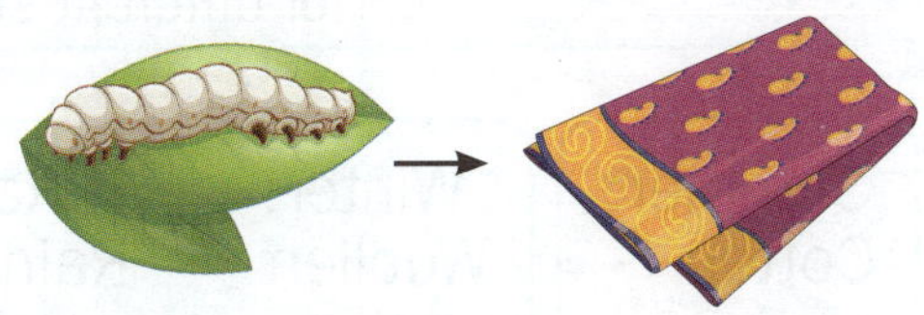
Silk from silkworms is used to make silk clothes.

LOOKING AFTER OUR CLOTHES

We must always keep our clothes clean. Here are some ways in which we can look after our clothes.

- Cotton clothes should be washed and ironed regularly.
- Coats and silk clothes should be dry-cleaned.
- Woollen clothes must be washed separately or dry-cleaned and kept with naphthalene balls once winter is over.

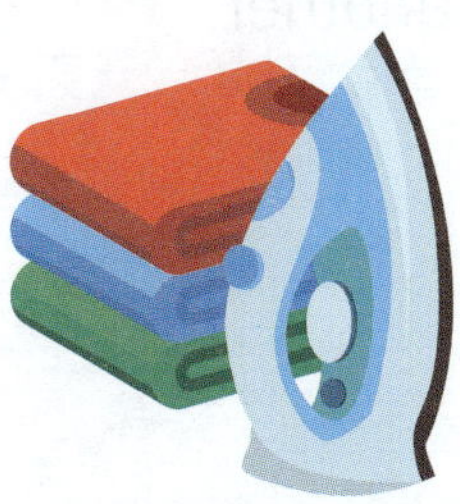
Ironing clothes

Dry wash

Naphthalene balls kept between clothes

We look and feel good by wearing clean and ironed clothes.

Concept Map

- **Houses**
  - types
    - Permanent
      - Strong houses
      - Examples: Bungalow, cottage, apartment
    - Temporary
      - Can be moved
      - Examples: Tents, yurts, caravans, houseboats
    - Houses in special places
      - Sloping roofs
      - Houses on stilts
      - Igloo
- **Clothes**
  - Types of clothes
    - for different seasons
      - Summer: Cotton clothes
      - Winter: Woollen clothes
      - Rainy: Raincoats, gumboots
  - are made up of
    - Fibres
      - types
        - Natural
          - Come from plants and animals
          - Examples: Cotton, jute, wool, silk
        - Artificial
          - Made by humans
          - Examples: Nylon, rayon, polyester, terylene

Summary

a. In this chapter, I have learnt that

- There are *pucca* houses and *kutcha* houses.
- Permanent houses cannot be moved from one place to another.
- We must keep our houses clean and free from germs.
- There are two kinds of fibres: natural and artificial.

b. I can do the following:

- Help my mother in keeping the house clean
- Wear clean and ironed clothes
- Wear the right clothes in different climates

Practice ZONE

A. Write T for true or F for false.

1. A house keeps us warm during the summer season.
2. A caravan is a permanent house.
3. Houses in very cold places are built on stilts.
4. In summer season, we wear clothes made from wool.
5. Nylon is an artificial fibre.

B. Match the following.

1. Caravan	a. Woollen clothes
2. Rainy season	b. Floating house
3. Winter season	c. Gumboots
4. Houseboat	d. House on wheels

C. Give reasons for each of these.

1. Our school uniforms should be washed regularly.

____

2. We cannot wear woollen clothes in summer.

____

3. We should make sure that no water is collected in any dish.

____

D. Answer these questions in brief.

1. What are *pucca* houses?

____

2. What is an igloo?

____

3. What are the two kinds of fibres?

____

E. Picture Talk

Look at the pictures of things that we use to keep our homes, clothes and ourselves clean. Label them.

Mop	Toilet brush	Washing powder	Scrubber
Cloth duster	Bucket	Mug	Liquid soap

 ____________

 ____________

 ____________

 ____________

 ____________

 ____________

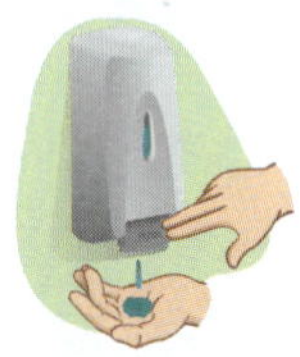 ____________

 ____________

F. Out of the box!

Paul's father is building a house in a region with heavy rainfall. What kind of house should he build?

____

____

Skills Enrichment ZONE

A. 21 CS Creativity and Innovation, Life Skills | AI | HQ Cooperation and Collaborative Living | 11 SUSTAINABLE CITIES AND COMMUNITIES

Collect ten empty match boxes and cover them with paper. Stick the boxes together with glue. Use these to make different kinds of houses. This activity can be done in groups. The class can design a whole city with different houses. Where do you live, in a city or a village? In which place would you like to live?

B. 21 CS Critical Thinking, Creativity and Innovation | AI | HQ Knowing My Needs

Mr Singh, the new Principal of your school, wants you to design your school uniform for the winter season. What type of fibre would you use to make the uniform and why? Draw and colour the uniform on a chart paper and display in your classroom.

Worksheet 5

STEAM CHALLENGE

Design a school uniform for summer using coloured paper or bits of cloths.

What is the challenge?

What supplies do you need?

IDEA 1

IDEA 2

What worked or did not work for you?

How can you improve it?

11 Transport and Communication

Prior Knowledge

In the previous classes, I have learnt that

- We use different means of transport to go from one place to another and to carry goods.
- There are three means of transport: land transport, air transport and water transport.
- Land transport can be of two types: road transport and rail transport.

Learning Objectives

In this chapter, I will learn about:

- Means of transport
- Communication
- Different ways to communicate

Let's Get Going

Rohit wants to travel to some other country. What means of transport will he use?

____

Sonal wants to travel from her town to her grandmother's town by land. How will she travel?

____

MEANS OF TRANSPORT

In Class 1, we learnt about the different means of transport. Let us revise them.

Land transport

Land transport is a means of transport that moves on land. Two types of land transport are—road transport and rail transport.

Real World

Some vehicles run on Compressed Natural Gas (CNG). Such vehicles do not give out smoke and do not cause any harm to the environment.

Some vehicles are pulled by animals or men, while others have engines that need petrol or diesel to run.

Bullock cart

Cycle

Car

Bus

Trains run on tracks and are the means of rail transport. Trains carry passengers and goods over long distances.

Electric train

Goods train

Air transport

When we need to travel very long distances such as from one country to another, we travel by an aeroplane. Aeroplanes and helicopters are means of air transport. They are the fastest means of transport. Helicopters can even land on places where there are no airports. These places can be open grounds or fields.

Your Task

Find out about the following means of transport.

a. Monorail
b. Bullet train
c. Glider

Aeroplane

Helicopter

Remember

The shelter under which an aeroplane is kept is called a hangar.

Water transport

Ship, rowboat, sailboat, raft, yacht, canoe, speed boat and ferry are the means of water transport. Ships carry people and **cargo** across seas to different countries.

Ship

Rowboat

Your Task

What do you call a ship that carries oil from one country to another?

COMMUNICATION

Communication means sharing of information, ideas and news. We can communicate with each other verbally or through **gestures** and signs.

My Dictionary

- **cargo:** goods carried by air, land and water transport
- **gesture:** a movement of a part of the body to express an idea or emotion

DIFFERENT WAYS TO COMMUNICATE

When we speak with each other, it is called **individual communication**.

When we need to spread information to millions of people together, we call it **mass communication**.

Individual communication

Speaking on phone, face-to-face talking, writing letters, sending personal e-mails and communicating through signs and gestures are the ways of individual communication.

Face-to-face talking

Through signs and gestures

Writing letters

Sending personal e-mails

Mass communication

In mass communication, a message is sent to several people at a time by using different means such as radio, e-mail, film, satellite news, magazine and newspaper.

Radio

Laptop

Television

Magazines

Newspaper

Books

Concept Map

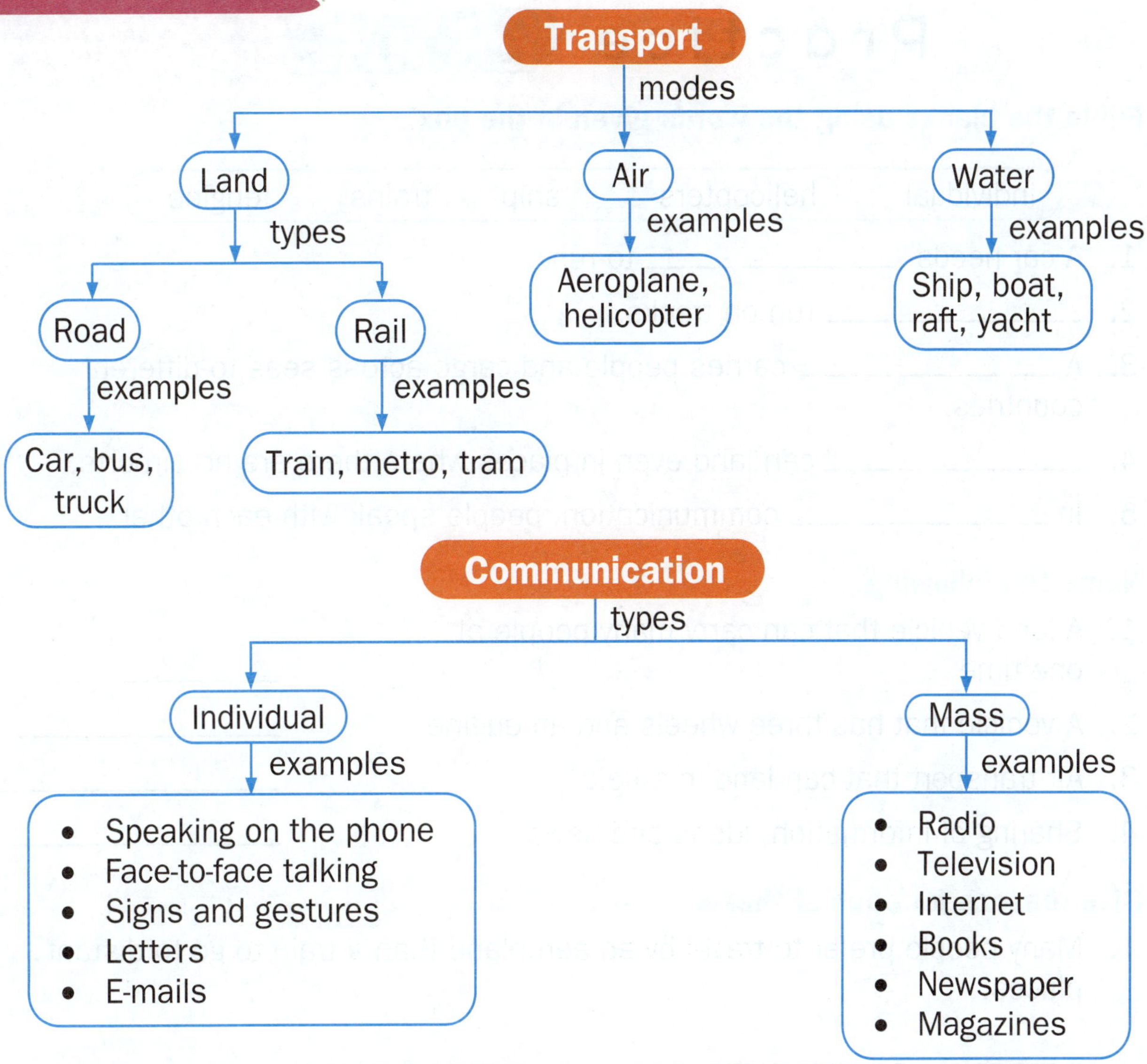

Summary

a. In this chapter, I have learnt that

- We can travel from one place to another by land, air and water.
- There are two types of land transport: road transport and rail transport.
- Communication means sharing information, ideas and news.

b. I can do the following:

- Name different means of transport
- Name different ways of sharing information

Practice ZONE

A. Fill in the blanks using the words given in the box.

individual	helicopters	ship	trains	engine

1. A car needs ________________ to run.
2. ________________ run on tracks.
3. A ________________ carries people and cargo across seas to different countries.
4. ________________ can land even in places where there are no airports.
5. In ________________ communication, people speak with each other.

B. Name the following.

1. A land vehicle that can carry many people at one time ________________
2. A vehicle that has three wheels and an engine ________________
3. Air transport that can land in a field ________________
4. Sharing of information, ideas and news ________________

C. Give reasons for each of these.

1. Many people prefer to travel by an aeroplane than a train to go to distant places.

   ____

2. Television is useful to students.

   ____

D. Answer these questions in brief.

1. List three means of water transport.

   ____

2. How do people who cannot speak communicate?

   ____

3. List three means of mass communication.

   ____

E. Picture Talk

Join the numbers and discover a mode of transport. You may add parts to it to make it your dream vehicle. Colour it.

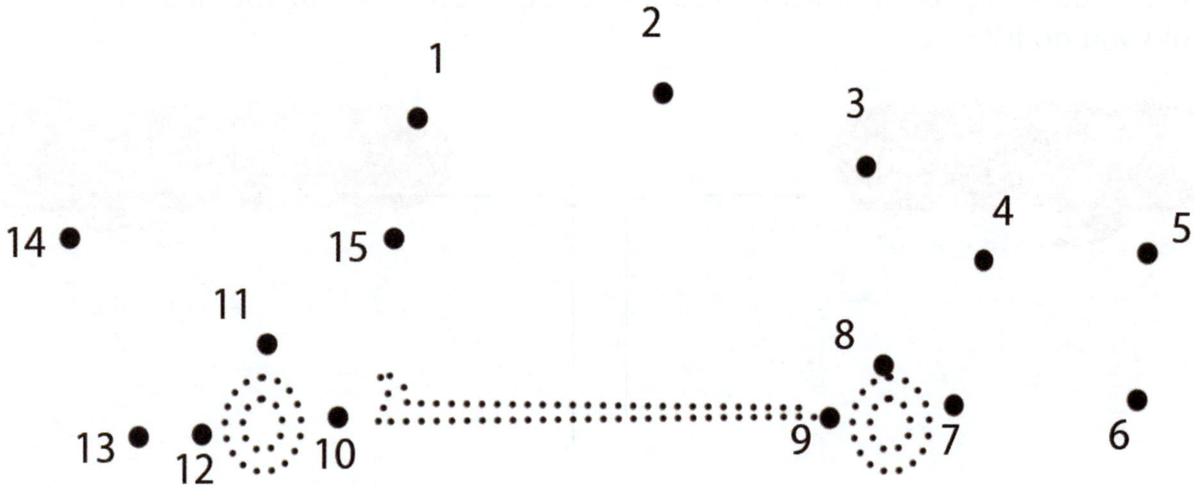

F. Out of the box!

Cyclone warnings are announced over television and radio. Why?

____

____

Skills Enrichment ZONE

A. 21 CS Creativity and Innovation | EL

Make a phone using string and paper glasses.

B. 21 CS Communication | CC Integration with English

9 INDUSTRY, INNOVATION AND INFRASTRUCTURE

Write a paragraph (5–7 sentences) to describe a recent journey through any mode of transport.

C. 21 CS Critical Thinking | CC Integration with English

Unscramble the letters to identify the means of transport.

1. licehterop ______________ 2. atxi ______________

3. rryef ______________ 4. naoce ______________

5. torocse ______________

Worksheet 6

STEAM CHALLENGE

How do people get daily news? If you had to send out news to your locality, how would you do it?

What is the challenge?

What supplies do you need?

1

2

What worked or did not work for you?

How can you improve it?

12 Air

Prior Knowledge

In the previous classes, I have learnt that

- We can feel air but cannot see it.
- All living things need air to live.

Learning Objectives

In this chapter, I will learn about:

- Air
- Wind
- What is air made up of
- Uses of air
- Air pollution
- How to keep air clean

Let's Get Going

AIR

Air is all around us. We cannot see it as it has no colour. We cannot smell it but can feel it. When we switch on a fan, we feel the air. All living things need air to live.

Your Task

Hold your palm close to your nostrils and breathe hard onto it. What happens? Do you feel something? Can you see it?

WIND

We feel air when it moves. You have learnt in Class 1 that moving air is called **wind**. Wind may be gentle or strong.

When wind blows gently, it is called **breeze**. Breeze is pleasant to feel. A strong wind is called **gale**.

A very strong wind is called **storm**. It may uproot trees and can cause damage to crops and properties.

Gale

Storm

Knowledge Check

Match the following.

1. Strong wind	a. Storm
2. Light wind	b. Gale
3. Very strong wind	c. Breeze

WHAT IS AIR MADE UP OF

Air is a mixture of gases such as nitrogen, oxygen and carbon dioxide, and water vapour. It also contains dust and germs. All living things breathe in oxygen and breathe out carbon dioxide. Plants use carbon dioxide to make food.

Talk About

What do you think will happen if you keep a sapling in an airtight container for a few days?

USES OF AIR

- All living things need air to breathe.
- Air is needed for burning.

Let's Try

With the help of an adult, light a small candle. Cover it completely with a glass. After some time, you will notice that the candle stops burning. This is because the glass cuts off the air supply. The candle burns as long as it can use the air in the glass and then extinguishes or burns out.

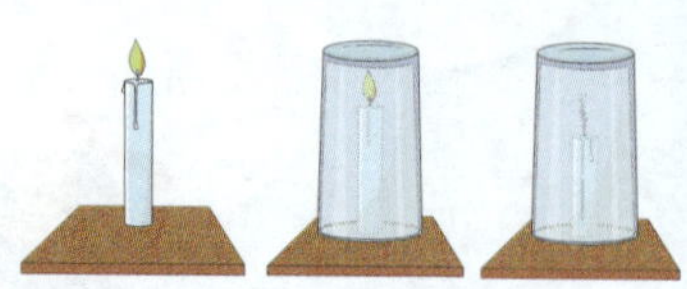

- Air is used for **inflating** balloons, footballs and tyres of bicycles, scooters, cars and buses.
- Moving air or wind helps yachts and sail boats to move.
- Wind helps in drying wet clothes.
- Wind is used to turn the blades of windmills.
- Wind helps aeroplanes, birds and kites fly.

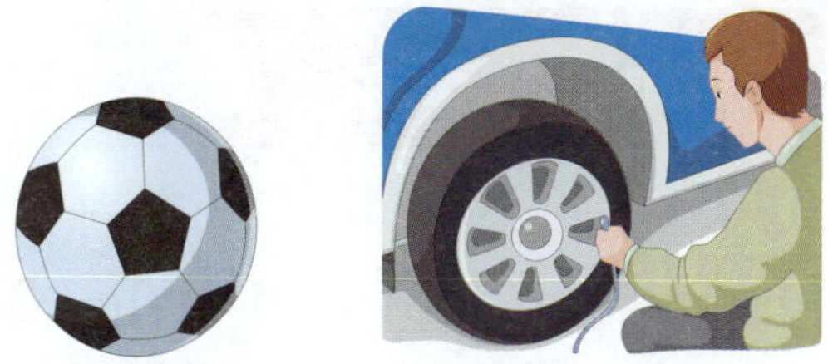

Air inflates a football and a car tyre.

Air helps an aeroplane and a kite to fly.

Wind turns the blades of a windmill.

Your Task

There is no air in space. Find out how space travellers survive in space.

AIR POLLUTION

Breathing fresh and clean air keeps us healthy. Sometimes the air around us gets dirty and causes air **pollution**. Dirty air makes us sick. It also affects animals and plants. Smoke from cars and of factories, presence of germs and dust and any kind of burning can pollute the air.

HOW TO KEEP THE AIR CLEAN

Here are some ways to keep the air around us clean.

- Plant more trees and stop cutting them down. Plants are natural purifiers as they produce oxygen that we need for breathing.
- Get our cars checked regularly for pollution. Walk or use a bicycle while going to nearby places.
- Avoid burning of crackers, plastic and rubber items.

My Dictionary

- **inflate:** blow up
- **pollution:** making the air dirty

Let's Try

Switch off all the lights and close all the curtains in the living room of your house to make it dark. Switch on a torch light. You will notice many dust particles floating in the path of the light rays of the torch. This shows that dust particles float in the air.

Concept Map

Air

- Gentle wind: Breeze
  Strong wind: Gale
  Very strong wind: Storm
- It is made up of gases such as nitrogen, oxygen, carbon dioxide, water vapour, dust and germs.
- Air has no colour or smell.
- Dirtying the air leads to air pollution.
- Uses of air
  - breathing
  - burning
  - filling balloons, tyres, football
  - moving sailboats
  - turn windmills
  - fly aeroplanes, kites, birds
- To keep air clean
  - Plant more trees
  - Cars should be checked for pollution
  - Avoid burning crackers, rubber and plastic

Summary

a. In this chapter, I have learnt that

- Air is all around us. All living things need air to breathe.
- Moving air is called wind.
- Air is made up of a mixture of gases, dust and germs.
- Dirtying the air results in air pollution.

b. I can do the following:

- Feel the air
- Take care not to dirty the air by burning crackers
- Grow more trees to keep the air fresh

Practice ZONE

A. Write T for true or F for false.

1. The tyres of a car need air. ☐
2. Gale causes a lot of damage to buildings. ☐
3. Air is made up of gases only. ☐
4. We can see air when we blow into a balloon. ☐

B. Fill in the blanks using the words given in the box.

air pollution	carbon dioxide	oxygen	wind

1. Moving air is called ________________.
2. All living things breathe in ________________.
3. Plants need ________________ from the air to make food.
4. Dirtying of air is called ________________.

C. Give reasons for each of these.

1. We should get our cars checked regularly for pollution.

   ____

2. We are harming ourselves by cutting trees.

   ____

D. Answer these questions in brief.

1. What is air made up of?

   ____

2. What causes air pollution?

   ____

3. Write a way to keep the air clean.

   ____

E. Picture Talk

Look at the glass tumbler. What do you think the glass tumbler contains?

____

F. Out of the box!

Why do you think an aeroplane cannot fly into space?

____

____

Skills Enrichment ZONE

A. 21 CS Critical Thinking, Information Literacy EL

Take two potted plants. Cover one completely with cellophane paper and leave the other as it is for a few days. Observe the plants and answer the following questions in your notebook.

1. What do you think will happen?
2. What do you see after a week?
3. Why do you think this happened?

B. 21 CS Critical Thinking EL

Take a piece of newspaper. Crush it tightly and fit it at the bottom of a glass. Turn the glass upside down and push it into a bowl of water.

Do you think it was easy to push the glass down into the bowl? (Yes/No)

Pull the glass straight up out of the bowl.

Touch the newspaper. How does it feel? (Wet/Dry)

Why does this happen?

C. 21 CS Creativity and Innovation, Life Skills AI

Make a poster asking your neighbours to keep the air clean. List the different ways in which this can be done.

13 Water

Prior Knowledge

In the previous classes, I have learnt that

- Rain is the main source of water.
- Water is needed for drinking, cooking, bathing and washing.
- We should never waste water.

Learning Objectives

In this chapter, I will learn about:

- Sources of water
- Uses of water
- Drinking water
- Forms of water
- Water cycle
- Saving water

Let's Get Going

Identify the water activities and write their names.

S________

F________

B________

All living things need water to live. Many animals spend their whole life in water. Without water, the Earth would become a dead place. So, it is very important to use water carefully.

Real World

When we sweat, we lose water from our body. So, we feel uncomfortable and thirsty.

SOURCES OF WATER

Rain

Places from where we get water are called sources of water.

Rain is the main source of all water. The other sources are ponds, lakes, rivers, seas and oceans.

Handpump

Some of the rainwater that falls on the ground seeps through the soil and gets collected under the ground. This is called underground water. We dig wells or use handpumps to get underground water. In some places, water gushes out from under the ground in the form of springs. At home, we get water from tap.

Let's Try

Take a paper cup. With the help of a pencil make a small hole in its bottom. Put some soil into it and place it in a tray. Now, pour some water on it. Leave it for a few minutes and observe what happens.

Talk About

- What is a dam?
- Why is it built?
- Name three things in which you store water at home.

USES OF WATER

We need water for our day-to-day activities. Water is used for drinking, cooking, washing, watering plants, bathing and as a mode of transport.

Real World

Water is used to produce electricity with the help of machines called turbines.

Drinking

Washing

Watering plants

Mode of transport

DRINKING WATER

We should always drink clean water. Sometimes germs or other things that we cannot see get mixed with water. Such water is unsafe for drinking and makes us sick. To avoid this, we must boil the water or use a water purifier or filter.

Your Task

Take some water in a glass and add some sand or soil to it. Take a piece of fine cloth or a strainer and pour the water through it. What do you see?

Real World

We cannot drink seawater as it is very salty. Seawater is treated in factories to make salt.

Knowledge Check

Answer these questions in brief.

1. What is the main source of water?

____

2. Write three uses of water.

____

FORMS OF WATER

Water exists in three forms—ice (solid), water (liquid) and steam or water vapour (gas). Water can be changed from one form to another by cooling or heating.

Ice Water Steam

Let's Try

- Take some water in an ice tray. Put it carefully into the freezer and take it out after two hours. What do you see?
- Leave the ice tray outside for an hour. What do you see?
- With the help of an adult, pour the contents of the ice tray into a kettle and place it on a stove. What is it that you see coming out of the spout?
- Hold a cold plate against the steam coming out. What happens to the steam?

The change in state of water also occurs in nature. Have you ever wondered what happens to the rainwater that forms little puddles on the road? Where does it go after some time? The heat of the sun changes it into vapour (the gas form of water) and it gets mixed with the air.

WATER CYCLE

The heat of the sun changes the water from oceans, seas, lakes, rivers and other water bodies into water vapour. This water vapour slowly rises above the ground. By coming in contact with the cooler layers of the air above, it converts into tiny drops of water. The drops of water join together to form clouds. When the clouds become very heavy, they fall as rain and again fill up the water bodies. This cycle goes on in nature all the time and is called the **water cycle**.

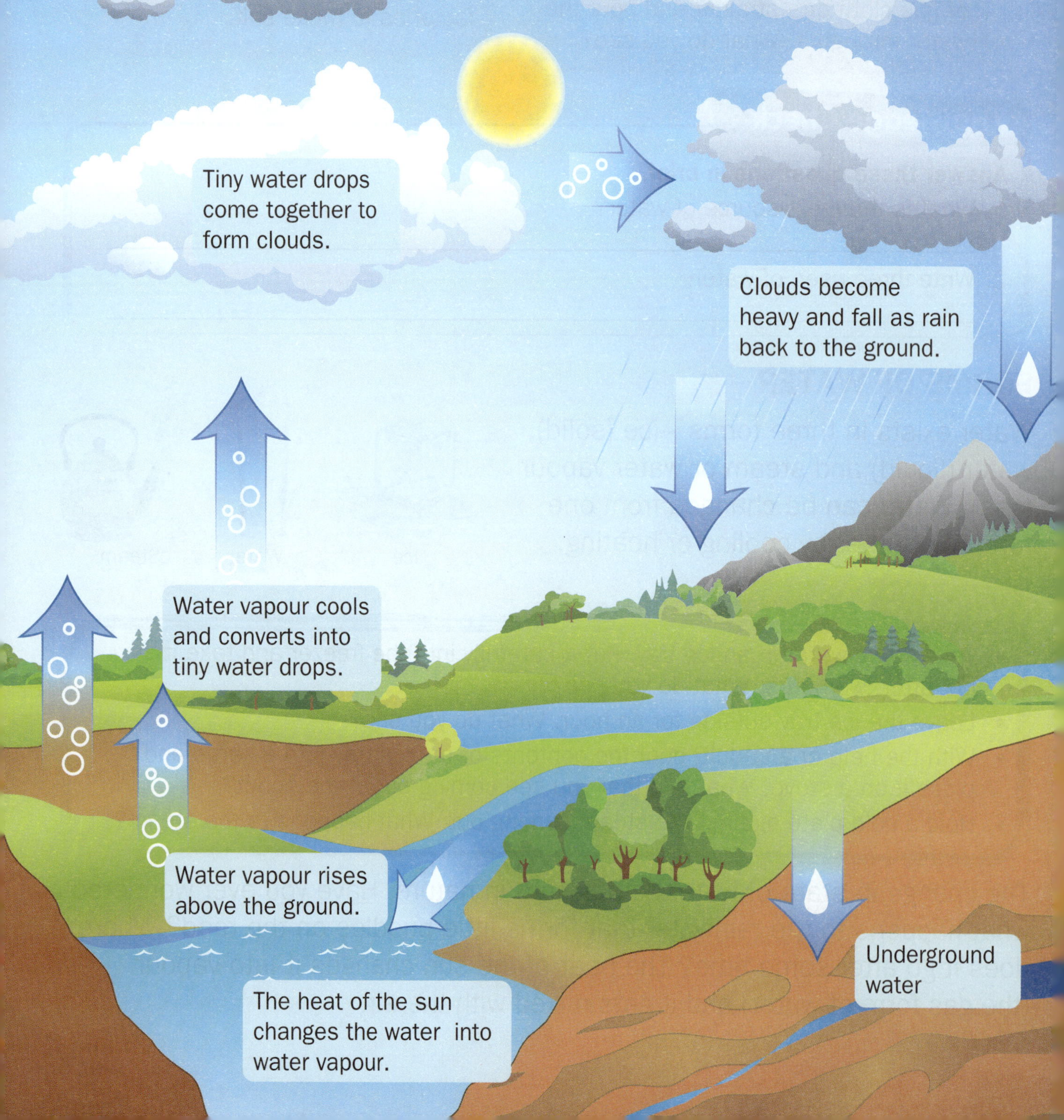

SAVING WATER

Water is very important for us and we should not waste it. Here are some ways by which we can save water.

- Do not keep the tap open while brushing your teeth.
- Close the tap tightly after use.
- Use a bucket and a mug to take a bath and avoid using a shower.
- Use leftover water from kitchen and bathroom to water your plants.

Concept Map

Water

- Sources of water
  - Rain
  - Ponds
  - Lakes
  - Rivers
  - Seas
  - Oceans
  - Underground water
- Uses of water
  - Drinking
  - Washing
  - Cooking
- Forms of water
  - Ice (solid)
  - Water (liquid)
  - Steam/water vapour (gas)
- How to save water
  - Do not keep the tap open while brushing.
  - Use a bucket and mug for shower.
  - Use leftover water to water plants.

Summary

a. In this chapter, I have learnt that

- Rain is the main source of water.
- We need water for drinking, washing, bathing, watering plants, generating electricity and as a mode of transport.
- Water exists in three forms—ice (solid), water (liquid) and water vapour (gas).
- In nature, water changes its forms in a cycle that is known as the water cycle.
- We should save water and use it carefully.

b. I can do the following:

- Name different sources and forms of water
- Save water by following various methods

Practice ZONE

A. Choose the correct option.

1. Steam is another name for ________________.

   a. ice b. water c. water vapour

2. The main source of water is ________________.

   a. ocean b. rain c. tap

3. We cannot drink water directly from a ________________.

   a. well b. sea c. river

B. Fill in the blanks using the words given in the box.

clouds	underground	boil	rain

1. Clouds become heavy and fall as ________________ back to the ground.
2. We dig wells or use handpumps to get ________________ water.
3. We ________________ the water to make it germ free.
4. Tiny water drops come together to form ________________ .

C. Give reasons for each of these.

1. We cannot drink water from the ponds without boiling or purifying it.

   ____

2. Water in the river becomes less in summer.

   ____

3. We cannot see the water from the water bodies going up to form clouds.

   ____

D. Answer these questions in detail.

1. What is underground water?

   ____

2. What makes water unsafe for drinking?

   ____

3. What are the three forms of water present in nature?

   ____

E. Picture Talk

Unscramble the letters to find the words related to water. Take hints from the pictures.

1. eic　　2. inra　　3. ahnpmdup　　4. lasgs

F. Out of the box!

We put wet clothes to dry outside in the sun. Where does the water go?

____

____

Skills Enrichment ZONE

A. 21 CS Critical Thinking　EL

Take four cups each half-filled with water. Add half teaspoon of each of the items to their respective cups as given in the table. Put a tick (✓) for the items that mix completely in water and a cross (✗) for those that do not.

Cups	Items	Does the item mix with water?
Cup 1	Salt	
Cup 2	Tea leaves	
Cup 3	Sugar	
Cup 4	Orange squash	

B. 21 CS Critical Thinking, Information Literacy　HQ Living in an Interconnected Society

14 LIFE BELOW WATER

Collect pictures and information on five living things found in water. Paste them on a chart and put it on display in your classroom.

14 Weather and Seasons

Prior Knowledge

In the previous classes, I have learnt that

- Weather changes from day to day.
- Weather is connected to the sun, wind and clouds.
- When the weather remains more or less the same for a few months, we call it a season.
- There are five seasons.

Learning Objectives

In this chapter, I will learn about:

- Weather
- Seasons

Let's Get Going

Match the pictures with the names of the seasons.

1. 

2. 

3. 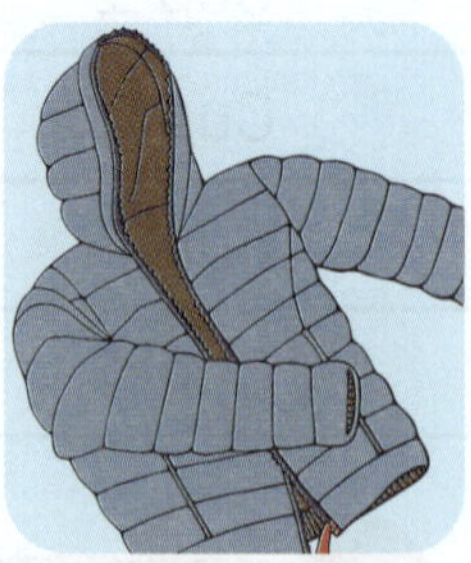

a. Spring

b. Winter

c. Summer

WEATHER

We know that the Earth is surrounded by a blanket of air called **atmosphere**. Sometimes, this air is hot and sometimes, it is cold. This change in atmosphere causes **weather**. Weather changes from day to day. It can be warm, cloudy, rainy, sunny or foggy. The weather of a place is determined by the sun, wind, rain and clouds. Weather plays an important role in our lives in how we dress, eat and plan our day.

Cloudy

Rainy

Windy

Sunny

Let's Try

Play a weatherperson and describe yesterday's weather. Talk about the weather today and predict the weather for tomorrow. Use words such as windy, hot, cold, stormy, cloudy, rainy, sunny, foggy, etc.

Do not forget to check if you were right in predicting the weather for the next day.

Knowledge Check

What kind of a day is it? The first one has been done for you.

1. A hot bright day sunny
2. When there is heavy rain with thunder ________
3. When the sun is hidden behind the clouds ________
4. A day when we can hardly see anything around ________

SEASONS

When weather remains the same for a long period of time, it is called **season**. In India, we have five seasons. They are summer, monsoon (rainy), autumn, winter and spring. Each season usually lasts for two or three months.

We wear cotton clothes in summer.

Summer

The summer months are the hot months. The sun shines bright and the days are hot. We like to stay indoors with fans, coolers or air conditioners switched on. During these months, the days are long and the nights are short. We wear light cotton clothes.

Summer makes us even more thirsty and we enjoy having cold water, juice and ice creams. Children enjoy swimming and we like to go to cool hill stations during our holidays.

Your Task

Find out the names of two seasonal fruits for summer.

Real World

Summer occurs because the Earth is slightly tilted (or bent) towards the sun.

Monsoon (rainy) season

After the hot summer months comes the monsoon season. During this season, the sky is often covered with dark clouds followed by rain and thunderstorms. The rainwater fills the dried-up ponds, rivers and lakes and forms puddles on roads. Farmers feel happy when it rains as it helps the crops grow. However, excess of rain can result in floods. We wear raincoats and gumboots and use umbrellas to protect ourselves from getting wet. Sometimes, we see a rainbow in the sky when it stops raining.

We wear a raincoat and gumboots in rainy season.

Trees shed their leaves in autumn season.

Autumn

Autumn is a short season that comes before winter. The days start getting cooler and the weather becomes pleasant. The leaves of trees often turn yellow as they dry up and fall on the ground.

Winter

In winters, the weather is very cold. The sun is not so bright and people like to stay outdoors to feel its warmth. The days are short and the nights are longer in winter. In some places, we see a thick cloud-like cover during early morning or evening. This is called **fog**.

We wear woollen clothes in winter.

People wear woollen or silk clothes to keep themselves warm. Some common items of clothing are sweaters or jackets, mufflers, long pants, gloves and woollen caps. People switch on the heaters and light fireplaces to stay warm. Everyone enjoys hot food such as soup during winter.

Spring

Spring is the season that comes after winter. It is very pleasant as the days are neither very hot nor very cold. Everything looks bright. The birds build nests, the flowers bloom and the butterflies **flit** about in the garden. People like to go for picnics in this season.

Flowers bloom in spring season.

My Dictionary

flit: move swiftly and quickly

Concept Map

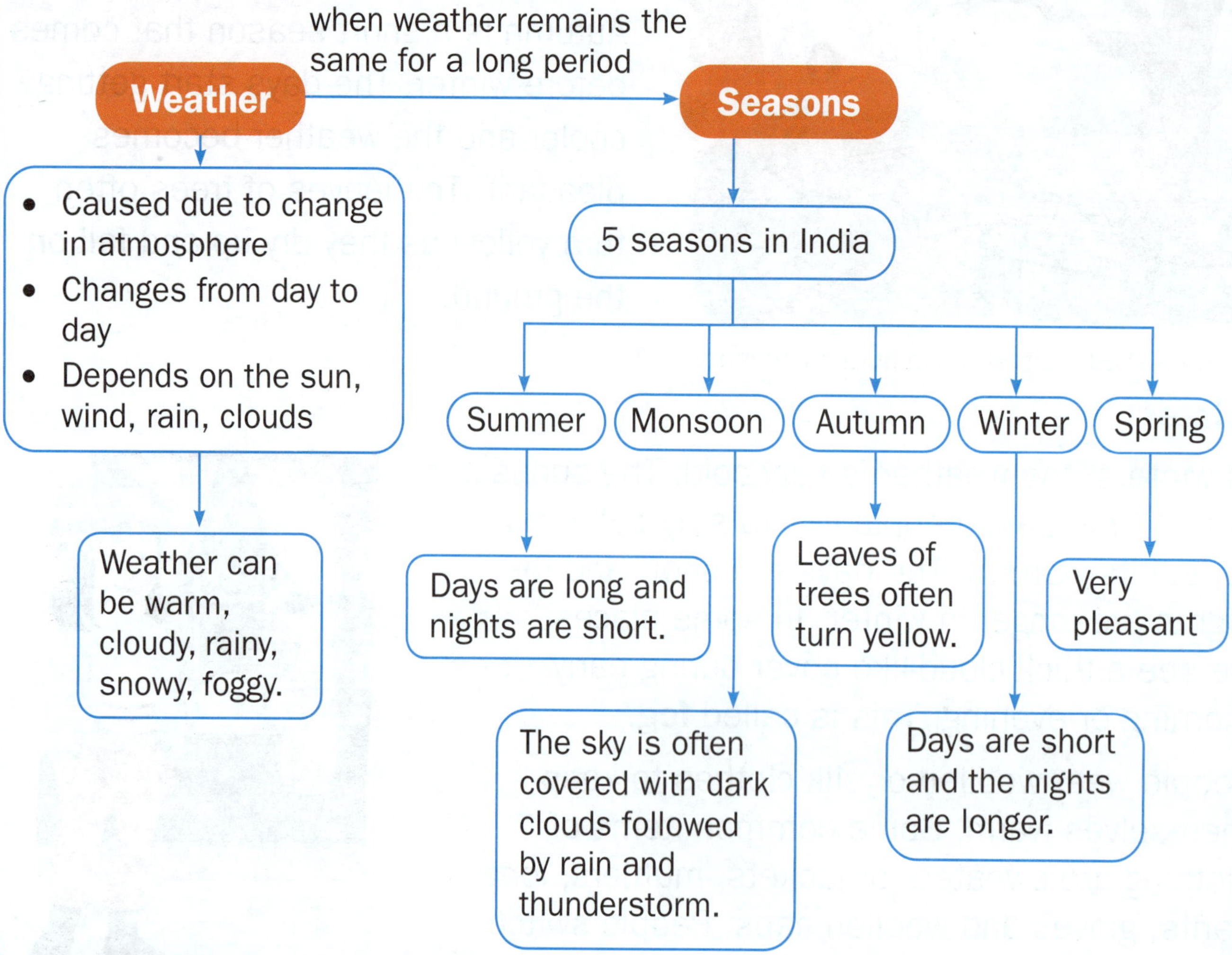

Summary

a. In this chapter, I have learnt that

- The change of weather is caused by the sun, wind, clouds and rain.
- Weather can be sunny, rainy, windy, cloudy, snowy or foggy.
- When the weather remains the same for a long time, it is called a season.
- There are five seasons: summer, monsoon, autumn, winter and spring.

b. I can do the following:

- Observe the weather changes from day to day
- Compare and explain the weather changes in each season
- Name the seasons and describe them

Practice ZONE

A. Write T for true or F for false.

1. Spring comes after winter. ☐
2. The sun shines brightly on a foggy day. ☐
3. The weather changes every day. ☐
4. We wear silk clothes in summer. ☐
5. The monsoon season is a dry season. ☐

B. Fill in the blanks using the words given in the box.

summer	winter	weather	woollen

1. ________________ changes from day to day.
2. Autumn comes before ________________ .
3. People wear ________________ clothes to keep themselves warm.
4. The ________________ months are the hot months.

C. Give reasons for each of these.

1. The weather may be sunny in the morning but cloudy in the afternoon.

   ____

2. People like to go for picnics in the spring season.

   ____

3. People light fireplace in winter.

   ____

D. Answer these questions in brief.

1. Name the factors that affect the weather.

   ____

2. What is a season?

   ____

3. What kind of food do you like to have in summer?

   ____

4. How do you prepare yourself for outdoors during monsoon?

____

E. Picture Talk

Sort out the words that go with the seasons.

Hill station Lightning Ice cream Rainbow Fireplace
Swimming Quilt Umbrella Hot soup

Summer	Monsoon	Winter

F. Out of the box!

Why is it important for fishermen to listen to the weather forecast?

____

____

Skills Enrichment ZONE

A. 21 CS Creativity and Innovation, Information Literacy AI

Have you seen weather symbols in newspapers or in TV news? Symbols that you see in the newspaper are shown here.

Make your own weather symbols for rain, snow, partly cloudy, thunderstorm and fog.

B. 21 CS Critical Thinking, Life Skills HQ Cooperation and Collaborative Living

What do you do with your old clothes?

Do you know many poor people do not have enough warm clothes to cover themselves in winters? What can you do to help these people?

15 Our Earth

Prior Knowledge

In the previous classes, I have learnt that

- The Earth is a living planet because it has both air and water.
- The land part of the Earth is made up of hills, mountains and plains.
- We find water on the Earth in seas, oceans, rivers, lakes, ponds and puddles.

Learning Objectives

In this chapter, I will learn about:

- Environment
- Different landforms on the Earth
- Water bodies on the Earth
- Keeping our Earth clean

Let's Get Going

Nature Walk

Go on a nature walk with an elder and make a note of five things that you see, smell and hear. Remember, all the things that you see, hear, smell or feel make up the world. Make a list in the space provided and share it with your friends. How many common things did you see?

Write all the things that you saw.

ENVIRONMENT

The Earth

Things around us form our **environment**. Many living things such as plants, animals and other creatures are found in our environment. The sky, mountains, hills, oceans, seas, rivers, ponds, valleys and deserts are a part of our environment.

You already know that the Earth is made up of land and water. In fact, three-fourths of its surface is covered with water and only one-fourth is land.

DIFFERENT LANDFORMS ON THE EARTH

The surface of the Earth is not the same everywhere. In some places, it is high while in some places, it is flat. These natural features on the surface of the Earth are called **landforms**. Let us learn about the different landforms.

Mountains

A mountain is the highest landform. It is in the shape of a cone with steep sides and a pointed peak that is generally covered with snow. A chain of mountains is called a range. The Himalayas is the highest mountain range in the world. Mount Everest is the world's highest mountain peak.

Mountains

Real World

Some mountains found under the sea may be taller than Mount Everest.

Hills

Hills are highlands but they are not as high as the mountains. Hills are generally covered with green trees and grass.

Hills

Valleys

The lowland between two mountains or hills is called a valley. Sometimes a river may flow through the valley.

Valley

Plateaus

Plateaus are flat-topped highlands. They look like a table, steep on the side and flat on the top. Thus, they are also called **tablelands**.

Plateau

Plains

The flatlands are called plains. It is easy to grow crops on plains as many rivers flow through them.

Plains

Deserts

Deserts are large sandy areas that receive little or no rainfall. Almost nothing can grow here and the only plants found are cacti and baobab trees. Very few people live in a desert.

Desert

WATER BODIES ON THE EARTH

Three-fourths of the Earth's surface is covered by water. We have already studied that water on the Earth is present in various water bodies such as rivers, lakes, seas and oceans.

Real World

- Cold deserts are large areas covered with snow. Antarctica is the world's largest cold desert.
- Pacific Ocean is the largest ocean in the world.

River

Sea

Ocean

Knowledge Check

Write T for true or F for false.

1. Three-fourths of the Earth's surface is covered by land and only one-fourth is water.
2. Only living things are a part of the Earth's environment.
3. It is easy to grow crops in flat plains.
4. We only find cacti and baobab trees in deserts.

KEEPING OUR EARTH CLEAN

Talk About

Which day is celebrated as the Earth Day and why?

Our Earth is a beautiful place, filled with the gifts of nature. We must take care of it and maintain cleanliness.

- We must keep our Earth green by growing trees.
- We must not litter and should throw trash in garbage bins.
- We must save electricity by switching off the lights and fans when not needed.
- We should save water by taking short showers or using a bucket and a mug to take a bath.
- Instead of taking a car, we should walk or use a bicycle while going to a nearby place.
- We must stop using plastic and carry a cloth bag when going to the market.

Boy planting a tree

Real World

We must follow the 4 Rs (Reduce, Reuse, Recycle and Recover) of environment to save the Earth. Find out the meaning of these terms.

Concept Map

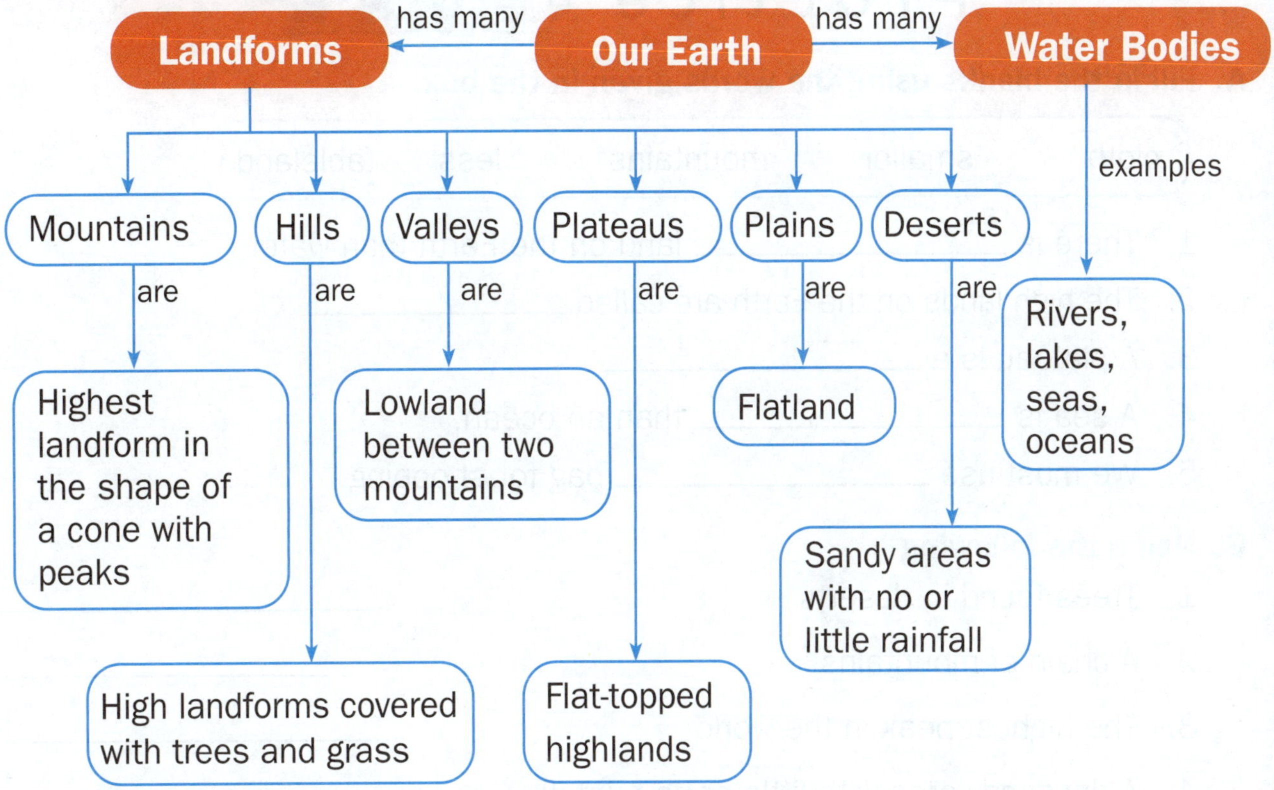

Summary

a. In this chapter, I have learnt that

- Mountains are the highest landforms. Hills are lower than mountains and plateaus are highlands that are flat on the top.
- Valleys are lowlands between two mountains or hills.
- Flatlands on the Earth are called the plains.
- Deserts are dry sandy areas with little rainfall.
- We must keep our Earth clean.

b. I can do the following:

- Identify the different landforms
- Keep the environment clean
- Plant more trees

Practice ZONE

A. Fill in the blanks using the words given in the box.

cloth	smaller	mountains	less	tableland

1. There is ____________ land on the Earth than water.
2. The high lands on the Earth are called ____________ .
3. A plateau is a ____________ .
4. A sea is ____________ than an ocean.
5. We must use ____________ bag for shopping.

B. Name the following.

1. Trees found in deserts ____________
2. A chain of mountains ____________
3. The highest peak in the world ____________
4. A dry sandy area with little or no rainfall ____________
5. Flatlands on the Earth ____________

C. Give reasons for each of these.

1. We should carry a cloth bag and not a plastic bag for shopping.

   ____

2. A camel survives in a desert without water.

   ____

3. Many people prefer to live in the plains.

   ____

D. Answer these questions in brief.

1. How much of the Earth's surface is water and how much is land?

   ____

2. What is a valley?

   ____

3. Write a way by which you can take care of our Earth.

   ____

E. Picture Talk

Take the trash to the bin to keep the Earth clean.

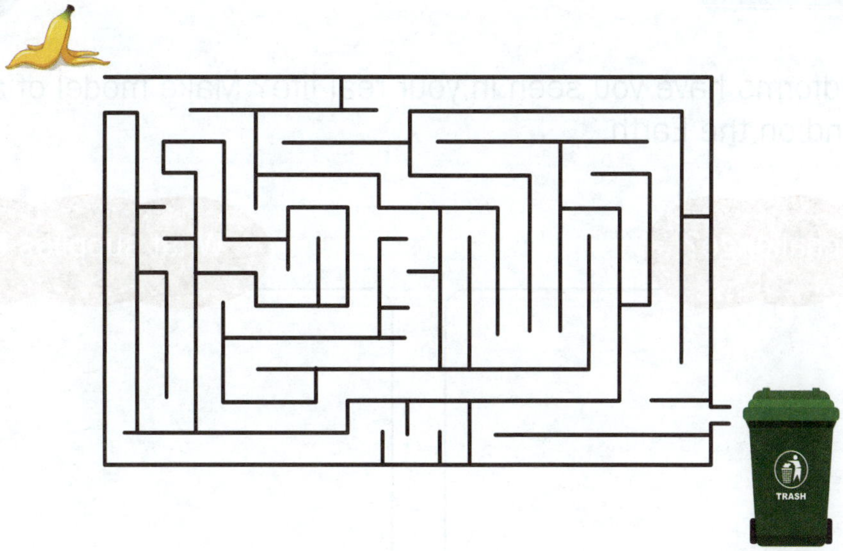

F. Out of the box!

More people stay in the plains than in the hills or mountains. What do you think is the reason behind this?

____

____

Skills Enrichment ZONE

A. 21 CS Critical Thinking, Life Skills

Find out the names of a mountain range, two hills, two rivers and a plateau in India. You may consult an atlas for this.

B. 21 CS Critical Thinking, Communication HQ Cooperation and Collaborative Living

Take a globe (a round model of the Earth). Select a place or a landform on it. Ask your friends to find it on the map. If they are able to find it, they score a point. Then your friends will ask you to locate a place. After eight rounds, find out whose score is the highest. The highest scorer will be the winner.

C. 21 CS Critical Thinking, Life Skills HQ Coexisting with Nature

14 LIFE BELOW WATER

Do you think throwing plastic bags into a water body is good? If we keep throwing plastics and other things into water bodies, what would happen to the living things found in the water?

Worksheet 7

STEAM CHALLENGE

How many landforms have you seen in your real life? Make model of any one of the landforms found on the Earth.

What is the challenge?

What supplies do you need?

1

2

What worked or did not work for you?

How can you improve it?

16 Rocks and Minerals

Prior Knowledge

In the previous classes, I have learnt that

- We see different kinds of rocks and stones around us.
- Stones are of different shapes, sizes and colour.
- Some stones are used as jewellery.

Learning Objectives

In this chapter, I will learn about:

- Rocks
- Types of rocks and their uses
- Minerals
- Types of minerals and their uses
- Gems or precious stones

Let's Get Going

Go to a nearby park with your friend and collect two stones each. Compare your stones with those of your friend's. Work together to find out how the stones are similar or different in terms of colour, size and shape.

Click a picture of your stones and paste in the frame given here.

ROCKS

The Earth is made up of hard substances called **rocks**. Rocks are found everywhere—on mountains and hills, under the oceans, on riverbeds as well as above and below the Earth's surface. There are different kinds of rocks. Some are hard and some are soft.

Sometimes the big rocks break down into smaller pieces. The pieces of rocks are called **stones**. Stones break down further to form a powder-like substance called **soil**. Plants grow in soil.

Types of Rocks and Their Uses

There are different kinds of rocks.

> **Real World**
>
> People who dig the earth for valuable substances are called miners.

Hard rocks

Rocks that are tough to break are called **hard rocks**. Granite, marble and sandstone are hard rocks.

Granite: Granite is a very hard rock. It is generally used as a building material to make floors and kitchen countertops. Granite can be grey, green or reddish-brown in colour.

Granite

Marble: Marble is used in buildings, statues and floors in homes. Marble is white, pink, grey, black or green in colour. The Taj Mahal in Agra is built from white marble.

Marble

Taj Mahal

Sandstone: Sandstone is softer than granite. It is mainly used in buildings. Sandstone is generally red but is also found in yellow, brown, grey and white colours. The Red Fort in Delhi is made of red sandstone.

Sandstone

Red Fort

Soft rocks

Some rocks are soft and can be broken easily. They are called **soft rocks**. Coal, chalk and slate are soft rocks. Coal is used as fuel for engines and cooking. Chalk is a soft white rock that is used to write on blackboards. Slate is a dark grey rock that is used to make blackboards. It is also used to build roofs of houses.

Coal

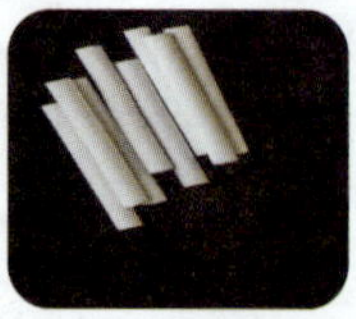
Chalk

Slate

Knowledge Check

Write T for true or F for false.

1. Granite is used as building material. ☐
2. Sandstone is harder than granite. ☐
3. Coal is a soft rock. ☐
4. Chalk is used to make blackboards. ☐

MINERALS

Rocks are made up of minerals. Minerals have different colours, shapes and sizes. Some minerals are hard and some are soft.

Types of Minerals and Their Uses

Graphite: Graphite is used in pencil leads and helps write on paper.

Quartz: Quartz is used in making watches.

Rock salt: Rock salt is used while cooking and adds taste to food.

Talc: Talc is used to make talcum powder. It is the softest mineral.

Diamond: Diamond is the hardest mineral. It is used in making jewellery and is a very expensive mineral.

GEMS OR PRECIOUS STONES

Gems are stones that are dug out from the underground. They are **precious** and used in making jewellery. Ruby and emerald are examples of gems.

My Dictionary

precious: valuable

Emerald

Ruby

Your Task

Find out names of two or more gemstones.

Concept Map

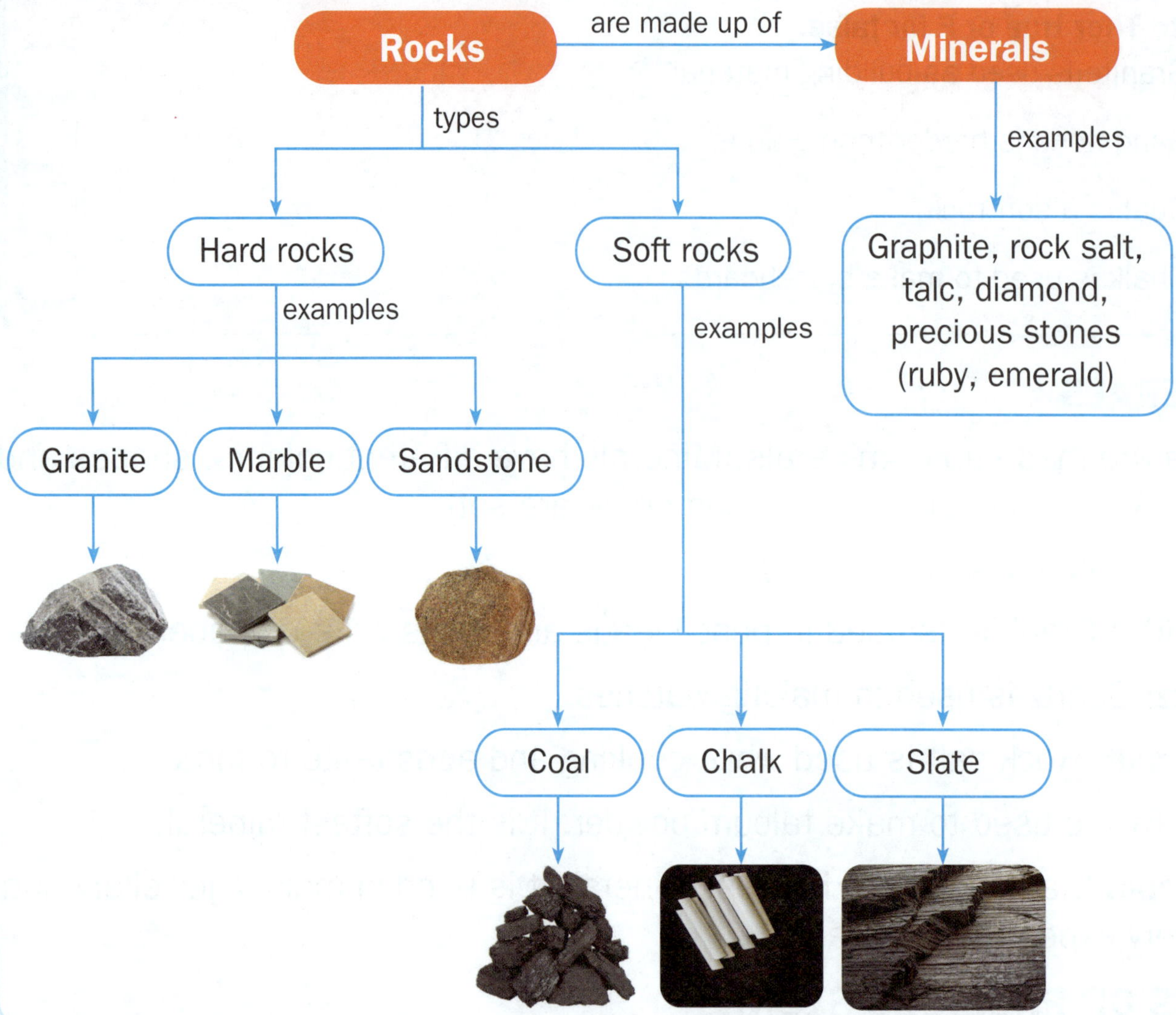

Summary

a. In this chapter, I have learnt that

- The Earth is made up of hard substances called rocks.
- Rocks are made up of minerals.
- Rocks can be hard or soft.

b. I can do the following:

- Identify the different rocks
- Identify the different minerals

Practice ZONE

A. Name the following.

1. I am built from marble. ____________
2. I am a mineral used in cooking. ____________
3. I am the hardest mineral. ____________
4. I am a mineral used in watches. ____________
5. I am a mineral used as talcum powder. ____________

B. Match the following.

1. Marble	a. Red
2. Ruby	b. Dark grey
3. Emerald	c. White
4. Slate	d. Green

C. Give reasons for each of these.

1. We cannot use slate to make the walls of our house.

   ____

2. Diamond is expensive.

   ____

3. Soil is important for the Earth.

   ____

D. Answer these questions in brief.

1. What are rocks?

   ____

2. Write the difference between hard rocks and soft rocks.

   ____

3. Write two uses of granite.

   ____

4. How do we get gemstones?

   ____

E. Picture Talk

Draw a soft and a hard rock in the boxes and name them.

____________________	____________________
Soft rock	Hard rock

F. Out of the box!

Rocks break down into smaller pieces over time. Name the things that bring about these changes.

____

____

Skills Enrichment ZONE

A. 21 CS Communication, Life Skills EL CC Integration with English

Find a rock and bring it to school. Along with your friends, conduct the following tests on the rock.

- Bring a magnet near it. Does it get attracted to the magnet? Yes/No
- Put it in water. Does it float/sink?
- Put it under a flash light. Does it shine or remains dull?
- Is your rock heavy/light?
- What is the colour of your rock? ______________

Based on the above information, write a description of the rock in your notebook.

B. 21 CS Critical Thinking

You have chosen a rock as a pet. Explain why it is easier to have a rock as a pet.

C. 21 CS Creativity and Innovation HQ Happiness My Goal EL

Collect different rocks and create a rock garden to beautify a lawn or balcony at your home.

17 Light and Shadow

Prior Knowledge

In the previous classes, I have learnt that

- We get light from the sun, moon, stars, bulbs, candles, etc.
- Light can pass through some objects.
- When we go out in the sun, we often see a shadow.

Learning Objectives

In this chapter, I will learn about:

- Sources of light
- Transparent and opaque objects
- Shadows

Let's Get Going

Tick the objects that give out light .

SOURCES OF LIGHT

Light helps us see things that are around us. We can only see things in the presence of light. There are different **sources of light**. Some sources are **natural** and some are **human-made**. The sun and stars are natural sources of light. They give out light of their own. All objects that have light of their own are called **luminous objects**.

Some of the human-made sources of light are electric bulbs, candles and lanterns. We can control a human-made source of light. For example, we can switch on or off a bulb. We can light or blow out a candle or a lantern. We cannot do that with a natural source of light.

Sun

Bulb

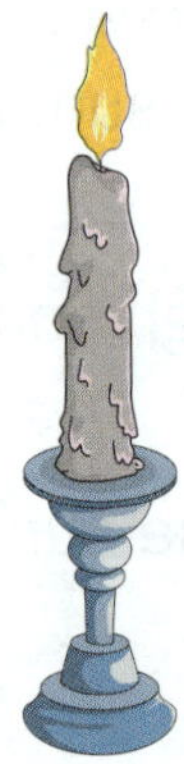
Candle

Lantern

Most objects around us do not have light of their own. We see them only when light falls on them. They are called **non-luminous objects**. Books, cupboard, the moon and trees are examples of non-luminous objects.

Moon

Real World

A glow-worm is a natural source of light.

TRANSPARENT AND OPAQUE OBJECTS

There are some objects through which light can pass easily. They are called **transparent objects**. Glass, water, air and cellophane paper are examples of transparent objects.

Glass

Book

The objects through which light cannot pass are called **opaque objects**. Books, wood and rocks are examples of opaque objects.

Knowledge Check

Give two examples for each of these.

1. Human-made sources of light ________________, ________________
2. Opaque objects ________________, ________________
3. Transparent objects ________________, ________________
4. Natural sources of light ________________, ________________

SHADOWS

A shadow is formed when light cannot pass through an object.

Facts about shadows

- A shadow is formed only when there is a source of light.
- A shadow is always black in colour.
- A shadow is always formed opposite to the source of light.
- The size of the shadow changes with the position of the sun. It is long in the morning and evening, but shortest in the afternoon when the sun shines above our head.

In the morning

At noon

In the evening

Let's Try

Go to a dark room and let your friend stand in front of you. Switch on a torch from behind. You will see that a shadow is formed on the opposite wall. Move closer to your friend and notice the change in the size of the shadow. Move away and notice the size again. Move in front of your friend. Do you still see the shadow on the wall?

Concept Map

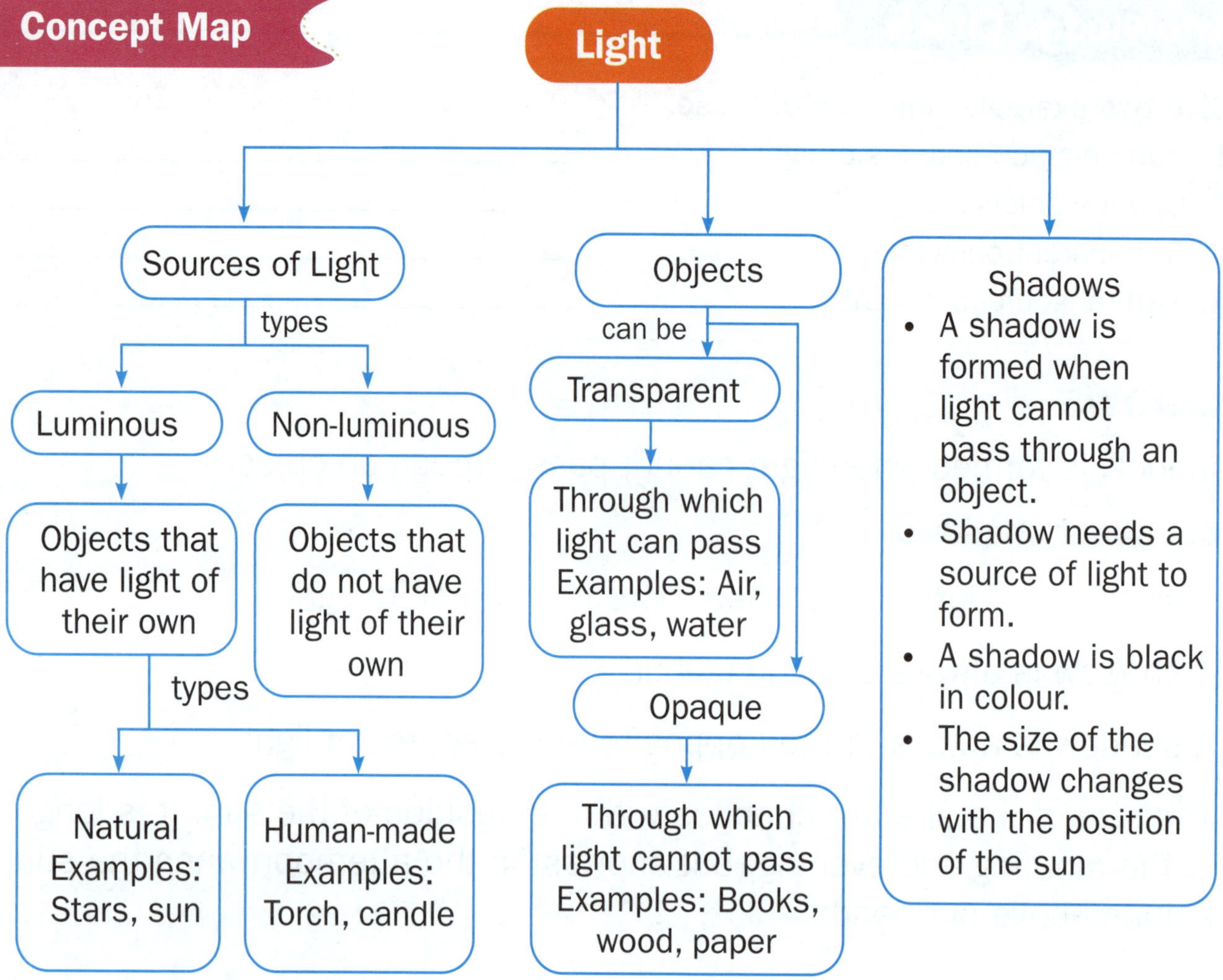

Summary

a. In this chapter, I have learnt that

- The sources of light can be natural or human-made.
- Objects through which light can pass easily are called transparent objects.
- Objects through which light cannot pass are called opaque objects.
- A shadow is formed when light cannot pass through an object.

b. I can do the following:

- Recognize different sources of light
- Form a shadow by flashing a torch over opaque objects

Practice ZONE

A. Fill in the blanks using the words given in the box.

sun	opaque	shadow

1. Light cannot pass through ______________ objects.
2. A ______________ is formed when light cannot through an object.
3. The ______________ is a natural source of light.

B. Write T for true or F for false.

1. A candle is a natural source of light. ☐
2. A shadow is formed on the same side as the source of light. ☐
3. A shadow is shortest at noon. ☐

C. Give reasons for each of these.

1. Some stars are bigger than the sun. But we do not get as much light from them.

____

2. The position of shadow changes throughout the day.

____

D. Answer these questions in brief.

1. Write any two sources of light. Give one example of each type.

____

2. How is a transparent object different from an opaque object?

____

3. How is a shadow formed?

____

4. Write a fact about shadows.

____

E. Picture Talk

Circle the correct shadow.

F. Out of the box!

Is the moon luminous or non-luminous? Why?

____

____

Skills Enrichment ZONE

A. 21 CS Communication AI EL

Go out to the garden early in the morning and observe the shadow of an object such as a tree. Draw an outline of the shadow with a chalk. Go back at noon and see if there is any change in the position of the shadow. Make an outline of the shadow again. Go back again after three hours and draw an outline of the shadow that is formed. Write your observations in your notebook.

B. 21 CS Critical Thinking, Life Skills

12 RESPONSIBLE CONSUMPTION AND PRODUCTION

What can you do to save electricity? Switching off the lights when not in use is one idea. What else can you do?

C. 21 CS Communication CC Integration with English

Recite this poem together.

When I go out in the sun,

I sometimes think it is no fun!

This little fellow follows me everywhere,

Growing long and short without any care!

My mom says, 'it is called a shadow'.

I ask her, 'Why does it always follow'?

My mom says, 'It likes the light'

Specially on a day that is bright.

But on a misty or a rainy day,

It behaves in a lazy way.

It does not come out of the bed.

'So, have fun', my mother said!

Worksheet 8

STEAM CHALLENGE

You know that rocks are used as building materials. What other uses of rocks can you think of? Some people decorate rocks as a hobby. What would you like to create using rocks? Create an interesting thing out of rocks.

What is the challenge?

What supplies do you need?

IDEA 1

IDEA 2

What worked or did not work for you?

How can you improve it?

Review Corner

Review 1 (Chapters 1–4) **(Maximum Marks = 25)**

A. Fill in the blanks. **(1 x 5 = 5)**

1. Small families are also called ______________ families.
2. We must ______________ our elders.
3. The name of my school is ______________.
4. The hard parts in our body are called ______________.
5. The ______________ covers our entire body.

B. Write T for true or F for false. **(1 x 5 = 5)**

1. Different members of a family must eat meals at different times. ☐
2. Family members support each other. ☐
3. Grandparents love to spend time with us. ☐
4. An adult human being has 209 bones. ☐
5. We should eat right food and exercise regularly. ☐

C. Give answers in one word. **(1 x 4 = 4)**

1. A place where two bones meet ______________
2. A picture of bones in our body ______________
3. Subject that teaches us about numbers ______________
4. School for very young children ______________

D. Answer these questions in brief. **(2 x 4 = 8)**

1. How is a small family different from a joint family?
2. Write four subjects you learn in school?
3. Write any two safety rules that should be followed on the road.
4. How can we keep our bones and muscles healthy?

E. Draw and colour the picture of your school. **(1 x 3 = 3)**

Review 2 (Chapters 5–7) (Maximum Marks = 25)

A. Fill in the blanks. (1 x 5 = 5)

1. ______________ is obtained from bamboo plants.
2. ______________ are made from *Aloe vera*, mint and garlic.
3. A ______________ makes paintings.
4. A ______________ sells fruits and vegetables.
5. ______________ is the harvest festival of Maharashtra.

B. Name the following. (1 x 5 = 5)

1. A plant that gives sugar ______________
2. A person who sells flowers ______________
3. The harvest festival of Punjab ______________
4. Festival of colours that marks the arrival of spring ______________
5. A person who lays electric wires and fittings ______________

C. Define the following. (1 x 4 = 4)

1. Herb ______________.
2. Trunk ______________.
3. Author ______________.
4. Architect ______________.

D. Answer these questions in brief. (2 x 4 = 8)

1. What do plants need to grow?
2. What is the difference between a creeper and a climber?
3. What is meant by occupation?
4. How is Bihu celebrated?

E. Identify the following festivals. (1 x 3 = 3)

1. 

____

2. 

____

3. 

____

Review 3 (Chapters 8–11) (Maximum Marks = 25)

A. Fill in the blanks. (1 x 5 = 5)

1. A ________________ is a bird that cannot swim but wade in water.
2. A rabbit lives in a ________________.
3. Animals that eat the flesh of dead animals are called ______________.
4. ________________ is sharing of information or ideas.
5. ________________ type of house has many storeys.

B. Choose the correct option. (1 x 5 = 5)

1. Which of the following is a wrong pair?

   a. Water transport b. Air transport c. Road transport
2. A bear eats ________________.
   a. only plants b. only animals c. both animals and plants
3. ________________ is a scavenger.
   a. Butterfly b. Mosquito c. Ant
4. Which of the following is a permanent house?
   a. Yurt b. Caravan c. Bungalow
5. Which of the following is a natural fibre?
   a. Cotton b. Nylon c. Polyester

C. Give one word for the following. (1 x 4 = 4)

1. Floating house made of wood ________________
2. Human-made fibres ________________
3. A harmful insect ________________
4. A plant-eating animal ________________

D. Answer these questions in brief. (2 x 4 = 8)

1. What helps a bird fly?
2. Name two ways of individual communication.
3. How do pets help us?
4. Write the difference between natural and human-made fibres.

E. Colour the picture of the given insect and label its body parts. **(1 x 3 = 3)**

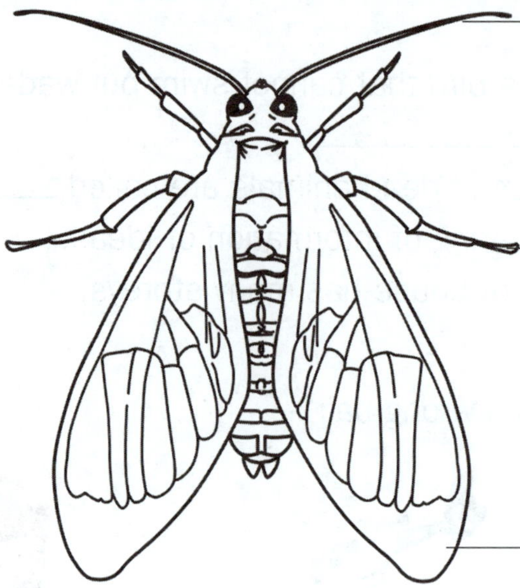

Review 4 (Chapters 12–15) (Maximum Marks = 25)

A. Fill in the blanks. **(1 x 5 = 5)**

1. The highlands on the Earth are called ______________.
2. ______________ is used to move the blades of the windmills.
3. Autumn comes before ______________.
4. ______________ is the main source of water.
5. When a strong wind blows fast, it is called ______________.

B. Name the following. **(1 x 5 = 5)**

1. A thick cloud-like cover during early winter morning ______________
2. Another name for water vapour ______________
3. The layer of air surrounding the Earth ______________
4. The season that comes after winter ______________
5. We cannot smell it but can feel it ______________

C. What kind of a day is it? **(2 x 2 = 4)**

1.

____

2.

____

D. Answer these questions in brief. **(2 x 4 = 8)**

1. Write two ways to keep the air clean.
2. What are hills?
3. What is underground water?
4. Name different seasons.

E. Label the diagram. **(1 x 3 = 3)**

Review 5 (Chapters 16–17) (Maximum Marks = 25)

A. Fill in the blanks. **(1 x 5 = 5)**

1. ________________ is the hardest mineral.
2. ________________ are stones that are dug out from the underground.
3. ________________ is a human-made source of light.
4. The shadow is shortest at ________________.
5. ________________ is used in pencil leads.

B. Write T for true or F for false. **(1 x 5 = 5)**

1. Fire is only human-made. ☐
2. We cannot see shadows at night. ☐
3. Diamonds are used for cutting. ☐
4. Soil is made from stones. ☐
5. A shadow is largest at noon. ☐

C. Sort out the hard rocks, soft rocks and minerals. **(1/2 x 8 = 4)**

Granite Graphite Marble Chalk Quartz Slate Coal Talc

Hard rocks	Soft rocks	Minerals

D. Answer these questions in brief. **(2 x 4 = 8)**

1. Write two facts about shadows.
2. What are luminous and non-luminous objects?
3. What is the difference between opaque and transparent objects?
4. Write differences between soft rocks and hard rocks.

E. Identify the types of rocks and write their names. **(1/2 x 6 = 3)**

____

____

____

____

____

____

Important Cities of India

Let us have a look at the important cities of India and their famous tourist attractions.

21 CS Information Literacy IF

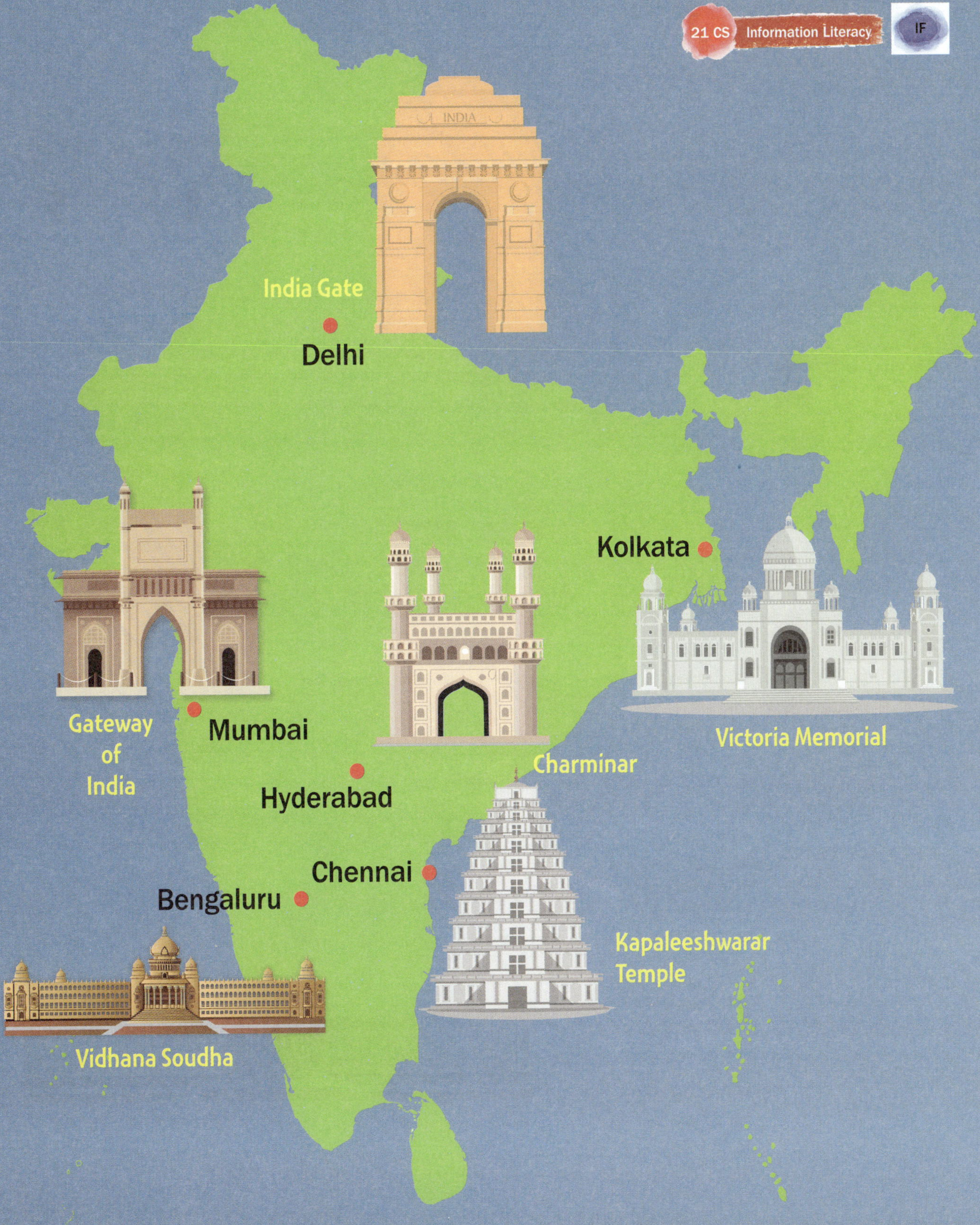

Delhi

Delhi is the capital of India. Delhi has various monuments that are famous in Indian history. Some of the most important tourist attractions in Delhi are India Gate, Qutub Minar and Red Fort.

Mumbai

Mumbai is the capital of Maharashtra. It is the place of origin of Indian cinema and film industry 'Bollywood'. Some of the most important tourist attractions in Mumbai are the Gateway of India and Marine Drive.

Kolkata

Kolkata is the capital city of West Bengal. It is crowned with various titles such as the city of palaces, the city of joy and the cultural capital of India. Some most important tourist attractions in Kolkata are Victoria Memorial, St Paul's Cathedral and Howrah Bridge.

Hyderabad

Hyderabad is the capital city of Telangana and Andhra Pradesh. It is also called the city of pearls. Some most important tourist attractions in Hyderabad are Charminar, Golkonda Fort and Ramoji Film City.

Chennai

Chennai is the capital of Tamil Nadu. Some most important tourist attractions in Chennai are Marina beach, Kapaleeshwarar Temple and Fort St. George.

Bengaluru

Bengaluru is the capital city of Karnataka. It is also known as the garden city because of its greenery. Some most important tourist attractions in Bengaluru are Vidhana Soudha, Cubbon Park and Mayo Hall.

CLASS

2

QUESTION PAPER SET

A

NSO

SOF NATIONAL SCIENCE OLYMPIAD 2020-21

DO NOT OPEN THIS BOOKLET UNTIL ASKED TO DO SO

Total Questions: 35 | Time: 1 hr.

Guidelines for the Candidate

1. You will get additional ten minutes to fill up information about yourself on the OMR Sheet, before the start of the exam.
2. Write your **Name, School Code, Class, Section, Roll No.** and **Mobile Number** clearly on the **OMR Sheet** and do not forget to sign it. We will share your marks / result and other information related to SOF exams on your mobile number.
3. The Question Paper comprises three sections:

   Logical Reasoning (5 Questions), **Science** (25 Questions) and **Achievers Section** (5 Questions)

   Each question in Achievers Section carries 2 marks, whereas all other questions carry one mark each.
4. All questions are compulsory. There is no negative marking. Use of calculator is not permitted.
5. There is only ONE correct answer. Choose only ONE option for an answer.
6. To mark your choice of answers by darkening the circles on the OMR Sheet, use **HB Pencil** or **Blue / Black ball point pen** only. E.g.

   Q. 16: Raj goes to school on a bicycle. Which of these safety rules he should follow?

   A. He should give signals before taking turns. B. He should keep to the right of the road.

   C. He should cross the road by using zebra crossing. D. All of these

   As the correct answer is option A, you must darken the circle corresponding to option A on the OMR Sheet. 16. ● Ⓑ Ⓒ Ⓓ
7. Rough work should be done in the blank space provided in the booklet.
8. Return the OMR Sheet to the invigilator at the end of the exam.
9. Please fill in your personal details in the space provided on this page before attempting the paper.

SOF

SCIENCE OLYMPIAD FOUNDATION

Inspiring Young Minds Through Knowledge Olympiads

Name:...

Section:............ SOF Olympiad Roll No.:.. Contact No.:..

1. Which of the following figures will complete the given figure pattern?

A.  B.  C.  D. Can't say

2. How many triangles are there in the given box?

A. 5 B. 7 C. 6 D. 8

3. Find the odd one out.

A.  B. 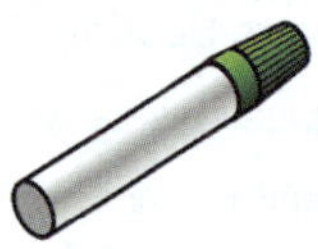 C.  D. 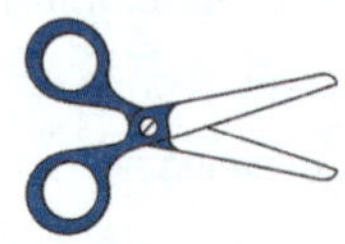

4. Monkey _______ is third to the left of second monkey from the right end.

(Left) K M T U P S L J

A. S B. P C. U D. M

5. Sneha's karate classes will start on the next day of third Friday of April 20XX. On which date will her classes start?

A. 18th April B. 19th April

C. 20th April D. 13th April

APRIL 20XX						
Sun	Mon	Tue	Wed	Thu	Fri	Sat
	1	2	3	4	5	6
7	8	9	10	11	12	13
14	15	16	17	18	19	20
21	22	23	24	25	26	27
28	29	30				

SPACE FOR ROUGH WORK

6. Refer to the given figure of a plant. Which of the following plant parts transports water, minerals and food to all plant parts?

A. P
B. Q
C. R
D. S

7. Read the given riddle and identify the animal.

- I can hop.
- I have a pouch.
- I have a long tail.
- My baby is called joey.
- Who am I?

A. Camel
B. Rabbit
C. Bear
D. Kangaroo

8. What will happen to a plant if we remove all the flowers from it?
A. It will not produce fruits.
B. It cannot stand upright on the ground.
C. It will stop transporting food and water to all other parts.
D. It will stop absorbing nutrients and water from the soil.

9. Anuj goes to the gym every day. After coming back from the gym, he eats eggs and fish at home. How do you think they help him?
A. They give him energy to do workout.
B. They protect him from diseases.
C. They help him in building muscles and bones.
D. They help him in preventing constipation.

10. Refer to the given relationship.

Creeper : Watermelon

Select the pair with similar type of relationship.
A. Climber : Pea
B. Shrub : Spinach
C. Herb : Money plant
D. Tree : Pumpkin

SPACE FOR ROUGH WORK

11. Refer to the statement given by Pawan.

Pawan

Which of the following sense organs is he using?

A. Eyes B. Nose

C. Ears D. Tongue

---

12. Which of the following is a living thing?

A.  B.  C.  D. 

---

13. Ali is very happy today. He is wearing new clothes and enjoying *meethi seviyan* made by his mother. Today is __________.

A. Christmas B. Eid C. Holi D. Diwali

---

14. 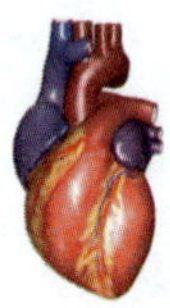 is an internal organ of the body. It helps to _______.

A. Think and work

B. Digest the food

C. Breathe air

D. Pump the blood to all parts of the body

---

15. Which of these is a National Festival?

A. Holi B. Christmas C. Gandhi Jayanti D. Diwali

---

16. Mira made the following pairs of food items, one each from plant and animal. Unknowingly she made a mistake while pairing them. Find the WRONG pair.

A. Soybean and honey

B. Egg and salt

C. Curd and rice

D. Chapati and chicken

---

17. Refer to the given conversation between Aditya and his mother.

Mother : Aditya, where are you?
Aditya : Mom, I am taking bath.

In which room of the house is Aditya present?

A. Living room B. Kitchen C. Dining room D. Bathroom

SPACE FOR ROUGH WORK

18. A copy of Rakesh's exam answer sheet is given here. Identify the mistakes he has made and select the correct option.

Fill in the blanks. **(5 Marks)**

(a) Never lean out of a moving bus or car.

(b) Never stand in a line while waiting for the bus.

(c) Never learn swimming in the presence of an adult.

(d) Always walk on the footpath.

(e) Always run while crossing the road.

A. (a) and (e) B. (b), (c) and (e) C. (b), (d) and (e) D. (a), (c) and (d)

19. Sheena's mother is making sweater from wool yarn as shown in the picture. What is this method called?

A. Weaving

B. Spinning

C. Knitting

D. Threading

20. Baby of the animal shown in the given picture is called a _______.

A. Lamb

B. Fawn

C. Foal

D. Joey

21. Select the vehicle that has the same means of transport as the one shown in the given picture.

A.  B.  C.  D. 

SPACE FOR ROUGH WORK

22. Refer to the given weather forecast report for 30th November. Which of the following is most suitable to be worn on this day?

A. Cotton shirt
B. Woollen sweater
C. Silk saree
D. Shorts

23. Which of these children follows good habits?
A. Avinash always obeys traffic rules on the road.
B. Deepa eats uncovered food from the vendors.
C. Suman always runs and plays in the corridors of her school.
D. Saira eats food that has fallen on the floor.

24. Ashish went to the market in a car and parked his car near a shop. When he returned after shopping, he was fined by the traffic police. He realised that he had not noticed the road sign of ________.

A. 
B. 
C. 
D. 

25. _________ causes day and night on Earth.
A. Earth's tilt on its axis
B. Rotation of Earth on its axis
C. Revolution of Earth in its orbit
D. Revolution of Moon around the Earth

26. Which of the following is mostly used for personal communication?

A. 
B. 
C. 
D. 

27. The given picture represents water cycle.
Which of the labelled parts represents processes:
(a) condensation and (b) evaporation?

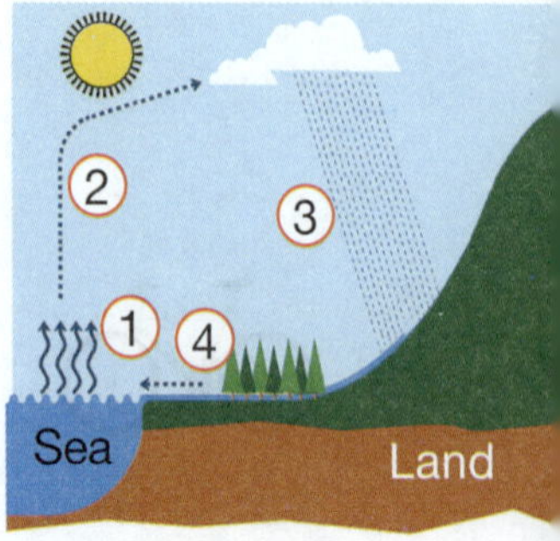

A. (a) - 1; (b) - 4
B. (a) - 1; (b) - 3
C. (a) - 2; (b) - 4
D. (a) - 2; (b) - 1

SPACE FOR ROUGH WORK

28. Select the correct match from the following.

A. Valley – Small low mountain

B. Pond – Still water

C. Plateau – Piece of land surrounded by water on all sides

D. Ocean – Freshwater

---

29. The given figure proves that ________.

A. Air gives shape to things

B. Air helps to move things

C. Air has weight

D. Air helps in burning

---

30. Which of the following is the shape of a Crescent Moon?

A.  B.  C. 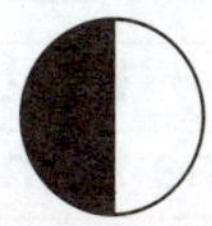 D. 

ACHIEVERS SECTION

31. Which of these children will NOT be able to differentiate between (1) Vinegar and sugar solution and (2) Red pen and blue pen?

A. 1 - Aman, 2 - Nakul

B. 1 - Puneet, 2 - Sumit

C. 1 - Puneet, 2 - Aman

D. 1 - Nakul, 2 - Sumit

---

32. Match the columns and select the correct option.

	Column I		Column II
(a)	Herbivore	1.	Crow
		2.	Giraffe
(b)	Carnivore	3.	Zebra
		4.	Bear
(c)	Omnivore	5.	Deer
		6.	Tiger

	(a)	(b)	(c)
A.	1, 6	2, 5	3, 4
B.	2, 5	3, 4	1, 6
C.	1, 3	2, 4	5, 6
D.	2, 3, 5	6	1, 4

SPACE FOR ROUGH WORK

33. Refer to the given classification chart and identify d, e and f.

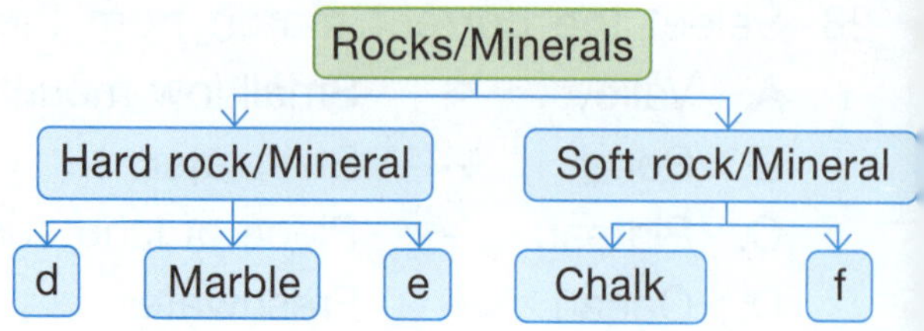

A. d could be talc while f could be quartz.
B. e could be granite while f could be sandstone.
C. d could be sandstone while e could be granite.
D. e could be graphite while f could be diamond.

---

34. Amrita is spending her holidays in Assam. She noticed that many houses there are raised on wooden poles. What can be the reason for this ?

A. Such houses are temporary and can be moved from one place to another.
B. Such houses are fire proof.
C. Such houses are built to collect water in drought prone areas.
D. Such houses are safe in areas where it rains a lot and which are flood prone.

---

35. Read the given table carefully about processes X and Y involved in water cycle.

	Features	Process X	Process Y
1.	It converts one form of water to another.	✓	✓
2.	It needs heating.	×	✓
3.	It needs cooling.	✓	×

Select the INCORRECT option regarding processes X and Y.

A. In process X, water may change from a gas to a liquid state.
B. In process Y, water changes from a liquid to a gas state.
C. Process Y will be slower on a warm day than on a cold day.
D. An example of process X is may be the formation of drops of water on the outer surface of a glass of ice water.

Eat Healthy, Stay Healthy!

His mother heard him cry and came running.
What happened?
Oh, my favourite shirt and jeans have shrunk. They don't fit me anymore.

If you want to fit into your clothes, you have to be healthy and eat lots of fruits and vegetables instead of only junk food.

Raghu started eating healthy food such as spinach, carrots, apples and bananas.
In a short time, he could fit into all his old clothes.
Mama, see the magic!
Moral: Eat healthy to be healthy and avoid junk food!

SEE Learning Social Emotional Ethical

Let's Save Our Forests!

21 CS Life Skills

HQ Coexisting with Nature

13 CLIMATE ACTION

My SEE (Social Emotional Ethical) Space

A. How does a forest fire affect the trees and animals living in a forest?

B. How would the Earth look if there were no forests?

C. Draw a forest in the space given below.

21 CS Creativity and Innovation AI EL

Earth Fair: Make an Ice Cream Stick House

A **house** protects us from heat, cold, wind and rain. It is made up of different building materials. Let us try making a house with ice cream sticks.

All You Need Is... Ice cream sticks, glue, scissors, cutter, paint brush and water colours

__Note:__ Do not use scissors or cutter yourself. Take help of an elder while cutting.

Let's Start!

1

Place two ice cream sticks parallel to each other. Also, place two more sticks on top of the first two forming a square. Glue these at the corners. Repeat this to build five more squares.

2

With the square placed flat, glue sticks in a line to cover the entire square. Repeat this to complete all six squares.

3

Now, take three sticks and glue them to form a triangle. Repeat the same process to make another triangle.

4

Stick both the triangles to one of the squares.

5

Now to cover the other side of the roof, glue these triangles to another square. Cut sticks and glue them across the open ends of the frame.

6

Cut a window and a door in the two different squares and glue them together to form four walls of the house.

7

Stick the roof onto the house and gently press down long enough for the glue to hold.

8

Use a paint brush to colour your house with different colours. Your ice cream stick house is ready!

Do It Yourself!

With the help of an elder, make a house using play dough. Write the things that you need and the steps of its construction. Draw or paste the pictures of the steps involved in the space provided.

All I Need Is: ____

____

____

____

Let's Start: ____

____

____

____

____

____

____

____

____

____

____

____

____

____

____

____

____

____

Eminent Personalities

Mary Kom

The first Indian woman boxer to win a Commonwealth gold medal

Shakuntala Devi

Indian mathematician who was known as the 'Human Computer'

Bachendri Pal

The first Indian woman to reach the highest peak, Mount Everest

Neeraj Chopra

The first Indian track and field athlete to win an Olympic gold medal in men's javelin throw

Subhash Chandra Bose

An Indian freedom fighter who led the Indian National Army

Dr Sarvepalli Radhakrishnan

A famous teacher who become the second President of India